Dublin Gray Indemnity Committee

The Power of Judges to Punish for Contempt of Court

As Exemplified by the Case of the High Sheriff of Dublin, 1882

Dublin Gray Indemnity Committee

The Power of Judges to Punish for Contempt of Court
As Exemplified by the Case of the High Sheriff of Dublin, 1882

ISBN/EAN: 9783337030841

Printed in Europe, USA, Canada, Australia, Japan

Cover: Foto ©Suzi / pixelio.de

More available books at **www.hansebooks.com**

THE

POWER OF JUDGES TO PUNISH

FOR

Contempt of Court,

AS EXEMPLIFIED BY THE CASE OF

𝔗𝔥𝔢 𝔥𝔦𝔤𝔥 𝔖𝔥𝔢𝔯𝔦𝔣𝔣 𝔬𝔣 𝔇𝔲𝔟𝔩𝔦𝔫,

1882.

PREPARED BY THE GRAY INDEMNITY COMMITTEE.

" The power ought not to be vested in any judge."—*Times*, March 17, 1875.

DUBLIN:

M. H. GILL & SON, 50 UPPER SACKVILLE STREET.

LONDON : SIMPKIN, MARSHALL & Co., STATIONERS' HALL COURT.

1882.

Gray Indemnity Committee.

——:-o-:——

THE RIGHT HON. THE LORD MAYOR (CHARLES DAWSON, M.P.).

MOST REV. DR. CROKE, Lord Archbishop of Cashel and Emly.

JOSEPH COWEN, M.P., Newcastle-on-Tyne.

JOHN DILLON, M.P.

HENRY J. GILL, M.P.

CHARLES S. PARNELL, M.P.

A. M. SULLIVAN, B.L.

GEORGE DELANY.

V. B. DILLON, Junr.

THOMAS MAYNE, T.C.

JOHN MULLIGAN, T.C.

JOHN NAGLE, P.L.G.

AMBROSE PLUNKETT.

ABRAHAM SHACKLETON, J.P., T.C.

ALFRED WEBB.

THE LORD MAYOR,
GEORGE DELANY, } *Hon. Treasurers.*

ABRAHAM SHACKLETON,
ALFRED WEBB, } *Hon. Secretaries.*

CONTENTS.

——:o:——

——:0:——

THE POWER OF JUDGES TO PUNISH FOR CONTEMPT OF COURT,
AS EXEMPLIFIED BY THE CASE OF THE HIGH SHERIFF OF DUBLIN. ·

"The power ought not to be vested in any judge."—*Times*, March 17, 1875.
(Cradock's Case).

——:o:——

ON August 16th, 1882, Mr. E. Dwyer Gray, M.P., High Sheriff of Dublin, and ex-Lord Mayor, was on the application of Mr. A. M. Porter, M.P., Solicitor-General for Ireland, summarily committed to prison for contempt of court by Mr. Justice Lawson then presiding at the Commission Court, for three months, fined £500, and ordered to find bail, himself for £5,000 and two securities for £2,500 each, to be of good-behaviour for twelve months, or in default to be imprisoned for a further term of three months.

In accordance with that sentence Mr. Gray was confined in Richmond Prison, Dublin, from that date until the close of the Commission on the 30th September, when Judge Lawson ordered his liberation on payment of the fine.

It is necessary to explain that this Commission, which was opened on the 3rd August, was the first under the provisions of the Prevention of Crimes Act. That Act made two new provisions for the trial of prisoners : it enabled the Attorney-General on his certificate to have the venue changed, and the prisoners tried by a special jury constituted under the Act, and it enabled the Lord Lieutenant to order prisoners, in capital and other cases, to be tried, if he so thought fit, by a tribunal consisting of three judges instead of by a jury. To this latter procedure it is well known that the Irish judges had the strongest possible objection. It is notorious that they urgently remonstrated with the Government against having such a duty put upon them, and that one of the most respected of their number, Baron Fitzgerald, resigned rather than undertake this new function. A number of prisoners charged with capital and other offences, committed in different parts of the country, were brought before this Commission, to be tried by a special jury under the Act, under the provisions for a change of venue by certificate from the Attorney-General. Amongst these were John O'Connor and others, charged with attacking a house, and Francis Hynes, charged with having committed a murder in the County Clare. The proceedings of the Commission were watched with great interest, and it was naturally assumed that if under the new arrangements the Crown failed to obtain verdicts, it would resort to the alternative provided by the Crimes Act, and require the judges to try such cases without a jury.

The contempt consisted in the publication of certain letters and comments in the *Freeman's Journal*, of which Mr. Gray is the proprietor.

They are given in full in the report of the proceedings in Court appended.

The event created considerable public excitement throughout Ireland, and was the subject of much discussion in the Press of the United Kingdom, America, and elsewhere.

In accordance with the practice, Judge Lawson communicated the fact of Mr. Gray's committal forthwith to the House of Commons, which was still sitting, and his letter was read by the Speaker to the House on the 17th August.

The Premier, in moving that the letter do lie upon the table, stated in effect that Parliament, which was about to adjourn the next day, was not in a condition then to deal with the matter or to refer it to a Select Committee, but indicated his intention to propose that it be so referred when the House reassembled.

In Dublin a committee was immediately formed to receive subscriptions to indemnify Mr. Gray for the fine of £500 imposed upon him. A larger sum was subscribed than was required for that purpose.

The Committee have considered that they could not better utilise portion of the surplus thus placed at their disposal than by placing the facts of this extraordinary case before the public in a more permanent and easily accessible form than can be secured by ephemeral newspaper reports.

They do so in the hope that a statement of this case may help to bring about some restriction of the right now claimed by judges to commit and fine for "contempt."

In the appendices will be found the full report of the proceedings, including the publications which constituted the alleged contempt of court, correspondence between Mr. Gray and Judge Lawson, between Mr. Gray and the Sub-Sheriff, between Mr. Gray and the City Coroner, into whose custody he was given on his committal, the jury panels analysed, and some other documents elucidating the case. The Committee also append notes of some cases of punishment for contempt in Great Britain which illustrate the extraordinary nature of the powers claimed and exercised by judges.

The Committee consider themselves justified in submitting the following considerations in connection with the case :—

The articles consisted of, first that published on the 11th August, stating that in the case of O'Connor and others the Crown exercised its right of challenge on a wholesale scale. This article was published the day after the case had concluded.

Another article, published on the 12th, with reference to the jury in the Hynes' case, complaining of the exclusion by the Crown of Catholics from the jury.

A letter from Mr. O'Brien complaining of misconduct on the part of some of the jury in the Hynes' case, and an article thereon published in the *Freeman's Journal* of the 14th.

A letter from Mr. Finucane, of Ennis, and a letter from Mr. Frost, the attorney for the prisoner, published on the 15th, complaining of the exclusion of certain evidence on behalf of the prisoner ; and a letter from Mr. O'Brien, published on the same day, confirming his previous letter.

The letter and article of which principal complaint was made, viz., those of the 14th August, were published after the trial was over, sentence passed, and the jury discharged. The Committee is unable to find any precedent for treating comments such as these on concluded trials as contempt of court, save only one created by Judge Lawson himself in the case of Mr. M'Aleese, a Belfast journalist.

The Committee do not believe that the publications constituted in law a contempt; but there is no legal means of testing this, for against a warrant of committal for contempt, if it be drawn up in legal form, it appears that no appeal lies, the judges of appeal invariably refusing to entertain any question of the legality of the sentence, and thus in such cases rendering a writ of *Habeas Corpus* unavailable. If Judge Lawson's contention be correct, to quote his own words when ordering Mr. Gray's liberation, "it seems doubtful if there is any other authority in existence which could deal with the matter." Thus, it would appear that the self-created powers of the judges supersede even the prerogative of the Crown. The Crown may pardon a murderer, but not, according to Judge Lawson, a man committed without having had time for defence, for " contempt."

Assuming that the publications were " contempt," the writers of the letters were amenable. One, Mr. Frost, was the defendant's solicitor, and of course, an officer of the court. Another, Mr. O'Brien, actually attended in court, avowed the authorship, and was desirous to testify on oath to the facts set forth in his letter, but by order of the judge he was summarily removed from the court. While the judge thus refused to entertain any evidence on behalf of the incriminated statements, which he avowed that he utterly disbelieved and treated as "inventions," and which he, as well as the Solicitor-General, stated could not be inquired into, he, in fact, speaking from the bench, disclosed that to a certain extent he had inquired into them, for he said (p. 53) that he "understood they were based on the hearsay of a waiter."

The Solicitor-General said that the truth or falsehood of the statements of Mr. O'Brien could not be inquired into. It appears, however, that the Crown Solicitor for Clare, Mr. Alexander Morphy, by whom he was instructed, had actually personally inquired into them two days before (see correspondence between the High Sheriff and the proprietor of the hotel, p. 72), and sat silent in court during the very time that the Solicitor-General stated that no inquiries could be made, and when the judge stated that he treated the statements as inventions, and sentenced Mr. Gray for publishing them. As a matter of fact the Attorney-General in the debate in the House of Commons, on the evening after Mr. Gray's committal, gave an undertaking that inquiry should be made into them, and subsequently the Lord Lieutenant did institute an inquiry into them, which was what the article in the *Freeman's Journal* asked for.

The statements of Mr. O'Brien were supported by a number of affidavits (eleven in all), sworn by visitors, waiters, and others who were in the hotel on the night in question. The committee understand that counter affidavits were subsequently sworn by members of the jury; affidavits were also sworn by the bailiffs and policemen in charge of the jury. As the committee have no means of procuring the counter affidavits of the jury, which have not been made public, they abstain from publishing the affidavits sworn in support of the statements contained in Mr. O'Brien's letter;

but most of them will be found in Hansard's report of the debate in the House of Commons on August 17, 1882. Whether these statements were true or false, or exaggerated, may have been of great importance in connection with the question of whether the capital sentence ought to have been carried out in the case of Hynes ; but they have nothing to do with the question of the propriety or impropriety of the sentence passed upon Mr. Gray, because the judge refused to inquire into the truth or falsehood of the statements in Mr. O'Brien's letter, so that whether they were literally true or absolutely false made no difference so far as the judge's view of Mr. Gray's offence was concerned.

Although, solely for the reason stated, the Committee refrain from publishing the sworn affidavits made in support of the allegations contained in Mr. O'Brien's letter, with reference to the amount of drink consumed by the jury, they print the letter of Mr. Hamilton, one of the jury, in which he gives a very different account of the matter. They also give the hotel bill and the summary of the affidavits of the bailiffs and police in charge of the jury.

But the separation of the jury and their mixing with the public is not questioned. The Committee, therefore, quote (page 65) portion of the affidavit of A. Martin, dealing with this particular matter, which, of course, is the most essential.

It appears to the Committee to be the manifest duty of a journalist to call public attention to alleged misconduct on the part of a jury, more especially when a human life is at stake. Assuming that a jury did misconduct itself—say, to take an extreme case, that it accepted bribes to give a false verdict what would be thought of a journalist who suppressed a letter accusing them of it, written by a correspondent whom he knew and in whom he had confidence ?

If the statements were false, the jury had their remedy by civil action or criminal indictment, so also had the Crown.

It has been argued that Mr. Gray, as High Sheriff, was responsible for the care of the jury. No doubt, he was nominally responsible ; but was he criminally responsible ? He had been in London for days before the trial. As is shown by the correspondence between him and the judge (p. 61), he had the judge's sanction for his absence. He spoke in the House of Commons on the Irish Postal Contract on the evening the jury was locked up, and did not return until after the jury were discharged. Nevertheless, Judge Lawson said more than once that he held Mr. Gray personally responsible for the care of the jury, although policemen and bailiffs were sworn by the court to take charge of them ; Mr. Gray was not in Dublin at all at the time.

Some English journals have gone so far as to suggest that Mr. Gray, as Sheriff, connived at the selection of a special hotel, which they call a Land League hotel, in order to entrap the jury, and that the whole affair was a conspiracy.

As a matter of fact, Mr. Gray left all these matters to the Sub-Sheriff, and knew nothing whatever about them. The hotel selected—the Imperial, in Sackville-street— is a very respectable one, situated in the principal street of the city. But in any case Mr. Gray had nothing to do with its selection. It was selected by the Sub-Sheriff, and the reasons of the selection are given in his letter.

Mr. Gray did not even make any special selection of his own Sub-Sheriff. This gentleman (Mr. James Campbell) is a well-known solicitor in Dublin, who has been Sub-Sheriff for a series of years. Mr. Gray selected him for this reason, and because he was warmly recommended by the late High Sheriff, Sir George Owens, a strong Conservative.

Although Mr. Gray was charged as a journalist, it is manifest, from the statements of the Solicitor-General and of the judge, that a portion of the criminal punishment inflicted upon him was in his capacity of High Sheriff. Notwithstanding this, the Lord Lieutenant did not comply with Mr. Gray's application for an investigation into his conduct as High Sheriff, though no steps have been taken to remove him from office, which, the Committee submit, should have been done if Mr. Gray were guilty of the acts imputed to him. (See correspondence, p 60).

Of course the High Sheriff might have been properly held civilly responsible for neglect or misconduct on the part of his subordinates, if such occurred, but this would have involved an acknowledgment of the charges which the judge called inventions.

In passing sentence, the judge did not discriminate between the various publications, but held them all to be in contempt. The Solicitor-General, after reading the article of the 11th August, declared that it, taken alone, constituted a gross contempt. It is submitted that that article is a bald record of fact which the liveliest imagination could not construe into anything more.

The opinion of Mr. Charles Russell, Q.C., M.P., and

Mr. Aspland, LL.D. (p. 27) show that the power of committal for contempt is practically unlimited and that there is no effective appeal against it.

It would appear that such is the extraordinary state of the law that if Judge Lawson had sent Mr Gray to prison for three years, or thirty years, instead of three months ; if he had fined him £50,000 instead of £500, or held him to bail for £1,000,000 instead of £10,000, there would equally be no legal remedy against so monstrous an injustice.

Although the question of the propriety or impropriety of the publications in the *Freeman's Journal* for which Mr. Gray was sentenced should be considered separately from that of the propriety or impropriety of the capital sentence upon Francis Hynes being carried out, still the Committee have deemed it desirable to append (p. 93) the memorial addressed to the Lord Lieutenant, by the prisoner's attorney, Mr. Frost, in which are quoted cases in which, when jurors separated, the sentences were not carried out, thus showing the vital importance of the questions raised in the publications constituting the alleged contempt.

Various other memorials were addressed to His Excellency, praying for the commutation of the capital sentence on Hynes, but they were unsuccessful, and on September the 11th he was hanged at Limerick.

The *Freeman's Journal* pointed out and it condemned the exclusion of jurors of a certain religious persuasion.

A tabular statement of the names of the jurors, drawn from the ballot box, to serve upon these particular trials, showing the religious persuasion of each, and indicating those ordered to stand aside by the representatives of the Crown and challenged by counsel for the prisoner, respectively, is appended.

An analysed list of the entire jury panel is also appended (p. 74). The letter of the Sub-Sheriff (p. 73) will show how this jury panel was drawn up. The procedure for the constitution of the jury panel is a purely mechanical one, and precludes all possibility of unfair selections. So, too, with the drawing of the names from the panel by ballot, to serve on any particular jury, which is a mechanical and necessarily absolutely impartial operation. But the Crown has an unlimited discretion to order jurors so drawn to "stand aside." Manifestly by exercising this power to a sufficiently large extent, it can by a process of exhaustion get a jury of a certain type, provided only twelve men of that type are on the entire panel after the prisoner has exhausted his challenges. How that power was exercised in Dublin at the late Commission will be seen by a reference to the analysis of the various cases.

There were four cases involving five trials of charges of an agrarian character at this Commission, under the Attorney-General's certificate for a change of *venue*. These were—O'Connor and others (the Kerry outrage case); Francis Hynes, murder ; Patrick Walsh, murder (two trials) ; and Michael Walsh, murder.

The analysis shows that while the entire jury panel contained 193 available names, of which 112 were Protestants, 80 Catholics, and one was a Jew—and while the names drawn to serve on the particular juries were in somewhat a like proportion, the Crown, by exhaustibly exercising its right to order jurors to stand aside, *excluded Catholics absolutely from every one of these juries.*

The precise number of Catholics ordered to stand aside cannot be ascertained, for in the case of the first trial of Patrick Walsh the jurors were ordered to stand aside by number and not by name, but the names are given of 66 Catholics, many of them of the highest respectability, ordered to stand aside in the other four cases ; and, as has been stated, not a single Catholic was permitted by the Crown to serve upon a single one of these five juries. With the exception of one Jew they were composed exclusively of Protestants.

The judge stated that the suggestion that men were excluded from sectarian motives was an atrocious one.

The Attorney-General, in the House of Commons, stated that he carefully abstained from inquiring into the religion or politics of any single individual member of the special panel, and his instructions, given to the Crown-Solicitor, were to take care that impartial juries be empanelled. " They did not know, nor did they hear anything as to their religion or politics."

But the facts speak for themselves. The Committee may be pardoned for quoting in justification, if any be needed beyond the facts themselves the charges of the *Freeman's Journal*, so indignantly repudiated by the Solicitor-General, that Catholics were excluded because they were Catholics ; the open declaration made by the *Daily Telegraph* of 3rd October, in a leading article. The *Telegraph* says, " We must, to convict murderers, secure, by hook or crook, by law or challenge, metropolitan Protestants and loyal juries," and the acknowledgment made in that same journal that there were "wholesale challenges," and that Catholics were set aside because of their supposed greater sympathy with agrarian crime. On juries empanelled to try other cases at the same Commission, Catholics were permitted to serve by the Crown; but the Committee cannot too strongly emphasise the fact that in every one of the agrarian cases every single Catholic was set aside and every single jury was composed exclusively of non-Catholics, and they refer to the analysed lists to show that this fact is beyond question.

It will be seen on examination of these lists that the jurors challenged by the prisoners were exclusively Protestants. These prisoners came from different parts of the country and were advised by different attorneys. They themselves could have had no knowledge, and it is probable that their attorneys had not much knowledge of the individuals composing the jury panel.

The fact of their challenges being Protestants is, however, very significant as proving that generally on the part of the accused and their advisers there was an impression that Protestants were likely to take a more unfavourable view of their cases than Catholics. Whether such an impression were true or false it emphasises the action of the Crown in excluding Catholics from every one of the juries, and so far as facts can prove anything it proves that the Crown took the same view. It is utterly impossible otherwise to explain away the fact of the Crown refusing to permit one Catholic to serve upon a single one of these juries.

In the Hynes case it so happened that one of the most important points on the trial was the exact significance and weight to be attached, as an evidence of the man's then mental condition, to the refusal of a Catholic priest to administer the Holy Communion to a dying man. It will readily be understood that Catholics and Protestants are not likely to take exactly the same view of or attach the same importance to a matter of this kind.

As to the statement of the Attorney-General that he was ignorant of the religion or politics of those set aside this may be literally true.

Before what is known as "Lord O'Hagan's Jury Act" was passed, jury packing had been brought to the perfection of a fine art in Ireland. But of course counsel for the Crown never had anything to do with it. It was the business of subordinates to see to the composition of the jury, and to be careful to keep their principals clear from all connection with or even knowledge of the proceedings adopted to attain the desired end.

The *Freeman's Journal*, in commenting upon public facts, had no means of judging the motives of individuals save from their public actions. It deduced from certain facts certain inferences, as it had a right to do, and it is submitted that these facts are incapable of any other inferences.

The statements made by a number of the jurors ordered to stand aside (page 88), shows that the same deduction was drawn by them. Any person resident in Dublin will know that these gentlemen are men of good standing and position, absolutely incapable of being false to their oaths. It is a curious fact that one of these gentlemen, Mr. Laurence Egan, who was lately a Town Councillor of Dublin, resigned his seat because he did not agree with his constituency that it was desirable to confer the freedom of the city upon Mr. Parnell, and was unwilling to occupy a representative position once his views and those of his constituency did not coincide.

It is submitted that it was not only the right but the duty of a public journalist to comment upon proceedings of the character described, and that such comments are calculated to maintain the impartiality of public trials and the consequent respect of the public for them. It is further submitted that comments upon the action of parties to a trial even if these parties be prosecutors, and even though the prosecutor represent the Crown, do not constitute in any real sense contempt of court. It can scarcely be argued that a Solicitor-General or a Crown Prosecutor can do no ill, nor can it be contended that the conduct of a jury is always irreproachable.

On the trial immediately following the publications in the *Freeman's Journal,* the procedure in court for the selection of the jury was changed. Up to that time, when the number was drawn from the ballot box, the name of the juror corresponding with that number was read aloud in court, and he was then either ordered to stand aside by the Crown, challenged by the prisoner, or sworn, as the case might be. But in the next case after this question of the exclusion of Catholics by the Crown was publicly raised, the number only was read aloud, and the Crown ordered the juror to stand aside without having the name declared in court The names of the jurors only who were not ordered to stand aside were read aloud, as they were being sworn, and thus the Press were not able in this case to ascertain the names of those set aside by the Crown. Subsequently the original system was reverted to.

With reference to the charges against the jury, it may suffice to repeat that all that was demanded by the *Freeman's Journal* was an inquiry by the Crown, and that the justification for that demand is to be found in the fact that the Crown felt itself compelled to institute that inquiry, and that the public attention and discussion which followed the article in the *Freeman's Journal* and the debate in the House of Commons elicited an acknowledgment from a member of the jury itself, that the jury had separated, and some of them had mixed with members of the general public. The question of the amount of drink which they may have consumed or the mental condition of some of them on the night of the 14th August appears of unimportance compared to this fact, which never would have been publicly known but for the letter and the article on account of which Mr. Gray was imprisoned.

The Committee have no desire to enter into any discussion with regard to the propriety of carrying out the capital sentence under these circumstances. They cannot refrain, however, from stating that they have been unable to ascertain any precedent for carrying out a capital sentence when it was proved that the jury had violated what has been called by eminent legal authorities "the sacred principle of inacessibility," and separated and mixed with the general public; while the memorial of the attorney for the prisoner, which is appended (page 89), shows that the practice in similar cases has been to commute the sentence even when there was little moral doubt of the guilt of the condemned man.

It is submitted that if the jury did misconduct themselves, or if there was reasonable grounds for believing that they misconducted themselves, or if any plausible accusation of misconduct was made against them, it was the duty of a public journalist to give it publicity in the interests of the pure administration of justice and of the respect due to it by the public. It is a common practice in England, once a trial is over and a verdict given, for the Press freely to comment on all the facts. It is also submitted that Mr. Gray was not bound, as was argued by the Solicitor-General and by the judge, to " suppress " publications in the _Freeman's Journal_ because he individually was High Sheriff. If this was the rule, independent journalists could never accept the office. The fact of Mr. Gray being High Sheriff should not be held to impose upon him limitations or conditions in the discharge of his duties in the conduct of his newspaper.

It would appear that at present there is no limit whatever to the power of a judge himself to decide what may or may not be contempt; that there is no definition of the offence which enables a public journalist to avoid it while exercising what is called the freedom of the Press; that the accused has no guarantee that he will be afforded an opportunity of defending himself, or bringing forward evidence either in his justification or in mitigation of punishment; and that there is no limit to the amount of punishment which may be inflicted upon him. Judges, after all, are but human, and no disrespect is intended by the Committee in pointing out that, like other men, they may be influenced, even unintentionally, by feelings of personal animosity, by prejudice, by heat or passion, by a wish to avoid having to discharge disagreeable duties, or by other motives innocent, perhaps, in themselves, but which, if carried to excess, involve injustice to the accused. Many sentences of contempt of court of the most bizarre and eccentric character might freely be quoted by the Committee.

In some cases it is almost impossible for the judge, who himself may have been the subject of attack which he feels himself bound to punish, or for the purpose of maintaining the respect due to his court, to avoid being influenced by personal feelings.

The Committee submit that, apart altogether from the merits or demerits of this particular case, apart from the question whether Mr. Gray deserved to be punished, and if so, whether his punishment was or was not proportionate to his offence, or whether he should have been given an opportunity of preparing his defence, if he had any, that the law regulating contempt of court requires, in the interests of public liberty, to be defined and limited, so that, while due security is provided for the unimpeded administration of the law and the maintenance of public respect for courts of justice, at the same time guarantees shall be given to all her Majesty's subjects against excessive and arbitrary punishment either by way of fine or imprisonment or the imposition of an excessive bail without the possibility of appeal. It is further submitted that the exercise by the judge of the power to remit portion of the sentence has nothing to do with the question of whether he was originally justified in imposing it, or whether such powers should be vested without any safeguard in any judge.

Most extraordinary mis-statements with reference to the action of Mr. Gray have been freely circulated in the English Press. The Committee would unduly extend the scope of this publication were they to review them at length ; or were they, on the other hand, to quote from the English, the American, and the Continental Press, as well as that of Ireland, articles and comments justifying and applauding his action.

As an indication of the feeling evoked in Ireland upon- the subject, it may be mentioned that all the Irish municipal bodies, except those of Belfast and Derry, passed votes of sympathy with Mr. Gray. Seven conferred their freedom upon him—44 Boards of Town Commissioners, 63 Boards of Poor Law Guardians, and 83 public bodies of various kinds also passed votes of sympathy ; not one public body passed a contrary vote, and in not a single case throughout all Ireland was a vote of sympathy defeated on a division ; but in several instances the chairman refused to put the motion.

If this case result in inducing Parliament to restrict a power which a reference to the cases 'quoted and the expression of public opinion thereon show to have long been nothing less than a scandalous abuse, Mr. Gray will not regret what he has had to undergo.

————:0:————

POWER OF THE JUDGES.
OPINION OF MR. CHARLES RUSSELL, Q.C., M.P., AND MR. L. M. ASPLAND, LL.D.

——:o:——

QUERIES ON BEHALF OF THE GRAY INDEMNITY FUND COMMITTEE,
FOR THE OPINION OF COUNSEL.

——:o:——

Q. (1.) In a case of alleged contempt of court is there any limit, and if so, what to, the punishment which a judge may inflict by way of fine, imprisonment, or bail?

A. We are of opinion that in the case of an alleged contempt of court there is no assignable limit to the punishment which a judge may inflict by way of fine and imprisonment. In re Clements v. Erlanger, 46 *Law Journal*, chapter 375, the Master of the Rolls said, " This jurisdiction of committing for contempt being practically arbitrary and unlimited, should be most jealously and carefully watched ;" and the authorities cited in exparte Fernandez, 10 C.B.N.S. 3, also 6 H. and N. 717, show that this description of the jurisdiction is correct. In the case of the county courts the power has been defined and limited by statute (Reg. Lefroy, L.R.S.Q.B. 134), but as regards the superior courts although it is said in Hawkins (2 Ph. cr. 4) that they may impose " reasonable" fines, it is for themselves alone to decide what fines are " reasonable."

Q. (2.) In the event of a person being sentenced to punishment by fine, imprisonment, or bail by a judge for an alleged contempt of court in a criminal case, has the person so sentenced any right of appeal, and to what tribunal?

A. We are of opinion that in the case supposed there is no right of appeal to any tribunal. In Burdett v. Abbot, 5 Dow.' 165, Lord Elden put to all the judges the following question— " Whether if the Court of Common Pleas, having adjudged an act to be a contempt of court, had committed for the contempt under a warrant stating such adjudication generally without the particular circumstances, and the matter were brought before the Court of King's Bench, by return to a writ of *Habeas Corpus*, the return setting forth the warrant, stating such adjudication of contempt generally, whether in that case the Court of King's Bench would discharge the prisoner, because the particular facts and circumstances, out of which the contempt arose were not set forth in the warrant ?" And the judges were unanimously of opinion that in such a case the Court of King's Bench would not liberate. And there are numerous authorities to the effect that the decision of the judge committing cannot be reviewed by anv other court. (Burdett *v.* Abbott, 14 East 1 ; Stockdale *v.* Hausard per Littledale, J. 9 A. and sec. 169; Carus Wilson's case per Lord Denman, cr. J. 7 Q. B. 1,008 ; exparte Pater 5 B. and S. 299). In general no appeal lies in such cases from the colonial courts to the privy council (Crawford's case 13 Q. B. 613, in re M'Dermott, L.R. 1 P.C. 200, 2 P.C. 651), although where it appeared on the face of the writ that the court had exceeded its jurisdiction (in re Ramsay, L.R. 3 P.C. 427) ; or if the offender had no opportunity of defending himself (in re Pollard, L.R. 2 P.C. 106) the Privy Council (acting under the wide power given by 3 and 4 Wm. IV., c. 41, s. 4, have advised her Majesty to remit the penalty ; but the rule that the exercise of the power of committing for contempt was not the subject of appeal was clearly laid down in M'Dermott's case L.R. 2 P.C. 341 where it is said (at p. 363), " Not a single case is to be found where there has been a committal by one of the colonial courts for contempt, where it appeared clearly upon the face of the order that the party had committed a contempt—that he had been duly summoned, and that the punishment awarded for the contempt was an appropriate one, in which this committee has ever entertained an appeal against an order of this description." See also in re Wallace, L.R. 1 P.C. 283. In re Fernandez, 10 C.B. N.S. 3 (Mr. Fernandez having been sentenced to six months' imprisonment and £500 fine), Erle. C.J. said, "We are not a court of review or a court of appeal—if Mr. Fernandez feels himself aggrieved by the course which has been pursued he may petition the Sovereign for relief ; but we have no power to question the propriety of what has been done." It is clear that the sentence in the present case is a judgment in a criminal cause or matter within the meaning of s. 50 of the Judicature Act 1877, and on that ground also it seems clear that no appeal lies. See Mellor *v.* Derham, 5 Q.B.D. 467 ; expte. Whitechurch 7 Q.B. D. 524 on the corresponding section of the English Act.

C. RUSSELL,
L. M. ASPLAND.

Temple, London, 30th September, 1882.

OPINIONS OF THE PRESS ON "CONTEMPT OF COURT."

———:o:———

THE following are comments of English Journals on some recent cases of contempt of court :—

CRADOCK'S CASE, MARCH, 1875.

At the Hertford Assizes for the, Spring of 1875, a man named Cradock was tried before Mr. Justice Denman, for passing bad coin and acquitted. The judge then sentenced him to twelve months' imprisonment for alleged contempt of court in a remark said to have been addressed by him to another prisoner in the dock. Cradock was pardoned by the Queen after a few days' detention.

" SATURDAY REVIEW," OF MARCH 27, 1875, SAID :

*   *   *   "And this brings us to the second question, as to the best means of dealing with persons charged with contempt of court, which is the more important of the two. The first consideration which suggests itself on this point is that, as everybody will allow, a man is always a bad judge in a case in which his own feelings or passions are likely to be involved. Even if he is able to restrain his personal prejudices or prepossessions he does not get credit for it, and there is always a tendency to suspect the impartiality of his decisions. It is true that in endeavouring to maintain the dignity and decorum of their courts, and in enforcing submission to such orders as they deem necessary to issue, the judges are acting, not for their own private interest, but for the good of the public ; but at the same time they are exposed to personal influences which may possibly lead them astray. There is, moreover, another ground on which objection may be taken to the present system ; and that is the inconsistency of dispensing in the case of an alleged contempt with the ordinary precautions of a trial before a superior court. In the instance of which we have already referred, Cradock had just as much right to all the securities for a careful and impartial trial when brought back on a charge of contempt of court as when he was originally placed in the dock on an indictment for passing bad money. In the one case he had the help of counsel, while the judge had the assistance of the jury. In the other he was surprised on the instant by an accusation of which he had had no notice, and had no one to advise him, and no opportunity of calling witnesses. Yet the one question was in every way just as serious as the other, and as much entitled to calm and patient investigation. The truth is—and it is a truth which is perhaps not sufficiently remembered, judges themselves occasionally forgetting it—that the grave persons on the bench, august and solemn as they look, are after all only men like the people about them, and subject to like impulses, and even, if we may be permitted to say it without contempt of court, like passions, with the rest of us. In London the dignity of justice is usually pretty well combined with the common sense of men of the world. The judges are surrounded by people who have known them all their lives, who are well aware that they have not undergone any supernatural transformation since they were at the Bar, and who are in the habit of calling them, when out of court, by names which identify them with the ordinary race of mortals. But there is some reason to fear that on circuit the javelin men and the trumpeters have a good deal to answer for, and that even the most sedate of judges is apt at times to feel as if he had just come from the clouds. There is no greater mistake than to suppose that judges do not require like other creatures of clay, to be protected against the weaknesses of humanity. As a rule English judges usually do their work very well, with scrupulous conscientiousness and virile intelligence ; but all judges are not exactly of the same stamp, nor always in the same mood, and it is for their own interest as well as for the interest of the community that too wide a margin should not be allowed for exceptional impulses. On every ground it is desirable that the power of inflicting punishment for contempt should be regulated on precise and settled principles, and it is to be hoped that the House of Commons will not shrink from the responsibility of dealing with the subject. It is enough that a judge should have power to order a person into custody without proceeding to try and sentence him on the instant."

THE "TIMES," OF 17TH MARCH, 1875, SAID :

"We do not say that Mr. Justice Denman was not acting at Hertford within his powers, but we do unhesitatingly say this—that the case proves that such powers ought not to be vested in any judge."

*　　*　　*　　*　　*　　*　　*　　*

" Mr. Charles Lewis called the attention of the Home Secretary yesterday afternoon to a report of the case and asked Mr. Cross how far he meant to interfere supposing the report in question was accurate. The Home Secretary, in his reply, gave a fuller version of the occurrence, but he admitted that a learned judge had summarily committed a person to prison for twelve months for contempt of court, and after detailing the circumstances of the case he added, that in his opinion, was not too severe. This may be true ; but we think it will be confessed by any one who reflects upon the matter, that 'the Home Secretary avoided the real point for consideration. The offender, who had been sentenced to twelve months' imprisonment, may have deserved this doom, but the question is whether the punishment ought to have been inflicted in the manner in which sentence was passed upon him. A man caught red-handed in a murder and lynched by an assembled mob may not have suffered a punishment too severe for his offence, but we should think very strangely of a Home Secretary who gave an opinion to this effect as his sole answer to a member calling his attention to such a swift execution of popular justice. The guarantees of personal liberty are at least put in peril if such a sentence as that, which was passed at Hertford, a fortnight since receives unqualified approval, and if judges are always masters of themselves so as never to give way to motives of impulse, they are still human beings, who must be, occasionally, capable of intellectual error.

*　　*　　*　　*　　*　　*　　*　　*

We do not say that Mr. Justice Denman was not acting at Hertford within his powers, but we do unhesitatingly say this, that the case proves that such powers ought not to be vested in any judge. We assume that the law warrants everything he did, and we are content to add that the law ought to be amended. Let us not be misunderstood. The act of threatening a witness or a possible witness in a trial with the intent to deter him from giving evidence bearing upon the issues of the trial is an offence against public justice which must be taken note of, and met with punishment by the laws of any civilized community ; but it is an offence which should be defined by the law, which should be proved like other offences before a jury ; and which should be visited according to a scale of punishment regulated by the law.

*　　*　　*　　*　　*　　*　　*　　*

Mr. Lewis gave notice yesterday, after receiving the Home Secretary's answer, that shortly after Easter he would call attention to the power of the judges to inflict fine and imprisonment without any appeal, and without any reference to a jury, for so called contempt of court. The notice is not given a moment too soon. The fact that those who have recently been visited with punishment for this offence have been persons, like Cradock, undeserving of sympathy, has led us to acquiesce in the exercise of an authority, pregnant with danger and not warranted by any sufficient cause. Those misdeeds which are now comprised under the general term of ' contempt of court,' are definable or they are not. If they are capable of definition, there is no reason why they should not be distinctly recognised in the Statute Book, and appropriate punishments provided for them. If they are so vague that their character cannot be clearly expressed in words, we must be excused for hesitating to give to the judges what according to this view is an unbounded jurisdiction accompanied by an indefinite power of punishment. The judges may have something to say for being allowed to retain the authority they have received from their predecessors, and if so, they should be invited to put it forward, the reasons hitherto advanced in extenuation of it being very unsatisfactory. Mr. Justice Denman has proved beyond a doubt that this is a branch of the law which demands inquiry."

" SPECTATOR," MARCH 20TH.

" It is impossible to deprive the judges of their power to make their procedure respected, but it is a power liable to abuse, and we do not see why it should not be subject to appeal. The sentence would then or at least be ratified by a judge who was not under the immediate influence of the contempt."

" SPECTATOR," MARCH 27TH.

" The Crown will be advised to pardon Cradock, and we hope the case will lead to a stricter definition of a crime which journalists have occasionally as great difficulty in avoiding, as in knowing when they have committed it."

" DAILY NEWS," WEDNESDAY, MARCH 17TH, 1875.

" Apart altogether from the particular case to which Mr. Charles Lewis, M.P., referred last night, there is probably a good deal to be said in support of his demand for an inquiry into the nature and limits of the power of judges to commit for contempt of court. No one, we presume, would argue that a certain amount of something like arbitrary power is not necessary for the judges in order to maintain that discipline and decorum without which Justice herself would sometimes have a poor chance of being heard. But this is a power the exercise of which every year of increasing civilization ought in the nature of things diminish, and, perhaps, therefore, to circumscribe. *   *   *

But, in the meantime, it may be reasonably argued that the present power of judges are somewhat indefinite, not to say anomalous. They seem to extend to many things that are not done or said in court, and to apply even to words and conduct which have only indirect reference to any trial going on in court. *   *   *   One peculiarity of the power to punish for contempt of court is that it enables the same person to be accuser, jury, and judge altogether. There are cases probably in which this is necessary and unobjectionable, but the principle is so peculiar that it needs more and more every day to have the limits and the purposes of its operation clearly defined."

" THE SCOTSMAN."

"The whole affair is apt to raise misgivings in the public mind, regarding this undefined power of sending people to prison without trial, for offences, real or imagined—the offence, the procedure and the sentence being all hurriedly developed on a moment's notice out of the judicial consciousness, at the time, perhaps in a state of excitement, irritation or anger.   *   *   *
It was a mere chance that Parliament was sitting at the time, and so secured a speedy release, otherwise Cradock might have lain weeks or months in prison. But whether contempt of court is to be disposed of summarily on the spot, or to be more deliberately inquired into, it is manifestly desirable that something more definite should be known about its nature and guilt. That ample protection should be afforded to all who aid in the administration of justice, whether as judges, pleaders, officials, or witnesses, will be readily admitted. Contempt of court, however, is mainly, if not entirely, designed, as the words indicate, for the protection of judges against disrespect or indignity when sitting in judgment, or against imputations on their integrity, or against disorders or interferences in court or out of it, calculated to obstruct or bias the administration of justice. In fact, a full power of self assertion is deemed neccessary to the efficiency, if not the very existence of a court of justice. It is impossible to dispute that some such power is necessary, and yet it is anomalous to have the execution of this undefined power committed to the discretion of those for whose benefit it is intended, who, therefore, practically become judges in their turn. Add to this the summary mode of inquiry and punishment by censure, fine, or imprisonment, and it certainly appears to us that there are special reasons for the principles and limits of this court, protecting law, being more clearly announced and defined."

" The resolution of which Mr. C. E. Lewis has given notice concludes in these terms :—' That, reserving the power of a judge to punish in a summary way whenever necessary, it is advisable to provide by legislative enactment that any person aggrieved shall have some right of appeal; and that when practicable, punishment for contempt of court shall be awarded only after trial, in due form and course of law.' This is the course adopted in France, and it saves the occupant of the judicial bench from figuring as prosecutor, witness, and judge conjointly and in his own case. Some such change, so far from weakening, would really strengthen the hands of the judges. It is no uncommon case for a judge to be defied and insulted in his own court because he hesitates to use the exceptional power with which he is armed. He would have no such hesitation in sending offenders before another and independent tribunal, while the mere knowledge that such a tribunal was available would have a miraculous effect in reducing the number of ' scenes' with which the public are now only too familiar."

THE "MORNING POST" (QUOTED IN THE "IRISH LAW TIMES," 20TH MARCH, 1875), SAID :

" Mr. Justice Denman will have rendered an immense service to the nation if the result of the recent committal of Cradock for contempt of court should be that a similar act is rendered impossible in the future."

THE " PALL MALL GAZETTE" (QUOTED IN THE "IRISH LAW TIMES," 20TH MARCH, 1875), SAID :

" We trust that the discussion in Parliament will induce the judges to set bounds for themselves to the authority which they at present exercise with respect to contempt of court. Arbitrary authority of any kind is a dangerous possession, and is apt to grow by invisible accretions in the hands of its possessors. It is only by the jealous supervision of those for whose ultimate benefit it is conferred, and by the wise self-restraint of those who wield it, that it can be preserved from degenerating into a scandal, if not an absolute instrument of oppression."

——:o:——

M'ALEESE'S CASE, MARCH, 1873.

" At the Antrim Spring Assizes of 1873, Mr. Justice Lawson sentenced Mr. Daniel M'Aleese, the editor of the *Ulster Examiner*, to fine and imprisonment for contempt of court in commenting upon a concluded case."

THE "DAILY NEWS" (QUOTED IN THE "IRISH LAW TIMES," OF
5TH APRIL, 1873), SAID:

"The severe sentence passed by Mr. Justice Lawson on Mr.
M'Aleese, of the *Ulster Examiner*, for contempt of court, will probably cause many persons to reflect how easily the powers
invented for their protection may be stretched too far. * * *
When Mr. Justice Blackburne sent Mr. Slapworth to prison, he
was careful to guard himself against the presumption that the
power of punishing for contempt is in any way intended for the
personal protection of the judges. Still less is it intended to
serve the purposes of repressing even the august criticisms of the
Press on a completed trial. The language attributed to Mr.
Justice Lawson would seem to imply that the continuation of the
assizes is pretty much the same thing as a pending cause. The
judge was even more unfortunate, if we may becomingly say so,
in imagining the assumed inaccuracies of the reports published
by the *Ulster Examiner* as a reason for exercising the powers of
the court, for mere reports published without permission may
as easily as false give rise to a process in contempt. The contempt, which consists in writing contemptuously of judges in their
judicial capacity, occupies no large space in the early law of the
subject, and it is a pity it should be allowed to increase. The
process as usually enforced is, as Blackstone says, ' not agree-
able to the genius of the common law; ' and we are sorry that
Mr. Butt's suggestion to proceed by indictment was not adopted.
Arbitrary justice is not much better in its effects than injustice."

——:o:——

POWELL'S CASE, AUGUST, 1874.

Powell, a cabman, was sent to jail for a week by a Welsh
county court judge for contempt of court.

"The *Law Times*, of 8th September, 1874, said—' The proceedings at Rhyl Sessions in which Mr. Vaughan Williams, a Welsh
county court judge, has figured so conspicuously and with so
little credit to himself, deserve more than the cursory notice
they have received. We have before us the *North. Wales Chronicle*
containing a verbatim report and the course of events was this—
Powell, a cabman, met the judge as he was going to the county.
According to the cabman he was on the road where he had a right
to be. According to the judge Powell was not where he had a
right to be and was in the judge's way. The judge requests
Powell to get out of the way, and when he did not do so, struck
him with the whip. There was, of course, conflicting evidence

as to the position of the parties, but the magistrates subsequently found the assault proved (a fine of £5 was inflicted on the judge). Before, however, they exercised jurisdiction over the case of assault, Mr. Williams, who was sitting on the Bench as a magistrate, saw Powell come into court and, without any inquiry, assumed to exercise jurisdiction under the 9th and 10th Victoria, c. 95, section 113.   *   *   *   Possibly at Rhyl the sessions are held in the same court-house as the county court, but Mr. Williams would hardly venture to rest his jurisdiction on such a flimsy pretence as that when he committed Powell for seven days—which imprisonment the unfortunate fellow has positively undergone—he was not sitting as a county court judge and could not avail himself of the County Court Act. The whole proceedings was, beyond doubt, flagrantly irregular and illegal."

—————:o:—————

REPORT OF PROCEEDINGS

IN THE

COMMISSION COURT, GREEN-STREET, DUBLIN,

AUGUST 16th, 1882,

BEFORE MR. JUSTICE LAWSON.

——:o:——

The Solicitor-General, Mr. A. M. Porter, M.P., rising said—
May it please your lordship—a matter was mentioned in court
on Monday which will have prepared your lordship for the application I am now about to make to the court, which is, my
lord, that an attachment may be issued against Mr. Edmund
Dwyer Gray, proprietor of the *Freeman's Journal*, in consequence of the publication of certain articles and other documents
in that newspaper reflecting upon the administration of justice
in this court, and calculated, in the opinion of those who represent the Crown, materially to interfere with the free exercise of
their duties by those to whom the administration of justice is
entrusted here. My lord, the notice of this application was
yesterday served, and I may as well state what that notice is.
It is addressed to Edmund Dwyer Gray, Esq., at the office of the
Freeman's Journal newspaper, in Prince's-street, Dublin—
"Take notice that at the sitting of the Commission Court, Green-
street, in the city of Dublin, on Wednesday, 16th August instant,
at 11 o'clock forenoon, counsel on behalf of the Attorney-
General will apply [to your lordship] that an attachment do
issue against you, Edmund Dwyer Gray, and that you be forthwith committed to prison for Contempt of Court, or such other
order as shall seem [to your lordship] fit. Such application
shall be grounded upon the affidavit of Alexander Morphy, intended to be sworn at the sitting of the court to-morrow, a copy
of which affidavit is herewith furnished you." Mr. Morphy has
made an affidavit, which is now sworn, and a copy of which, in
order to convenience Mr. Gray, was left with him yesterday in
order that he might not be taken by surprise by this application.
That affidavit is as follows.

433359

" I say that I am Crown Solicitor for the Counties of Clare
and Kerry, and as such Crown Solicitor I was professionally
engaged in the recent trials in the case of the Queen v. John
Connor, and others, for attacking the house of Mrs. Maybury,
and in the case of the Queen v. Cullen, for grievous assault, and
in the case of the Queen v. Francis Hynes, for the murder of
John Doloughty. Said trials respectively took place at the now
pending August, 1882, Commission, before the Right Hon. Mr.
Justice Lawson and special juries, under the provisions of the
Prevention of Crime Act, 1882. I say that the said Commission
is still pending, and other cases remain for trial thereat, before
special juries under the provisions of the statute. I say that I
have read in the issue of the newspaper called the *Freeman's
Journal*, published on Friday, 11th August, inst., an article commencing at the words ' Yesterday at the Commission,' and
ending with the words, ' Sentence was deferred.' I have also
read in the issue of the *Freeman's Journal*, published on Saturday, the 12th August, another article commencing with the
words, ' We are unwilling to credit the rumour,' and ending
with the words, ' Openly make such an accusation.' I have
also read in the issue of the said *Freeman's Journal* newspaper,
published on Monday, 14th August, instant, a letter purporting
to be signed ' William O'Brien,' and an article commencing
with the words, ' On Saturday Francis Hynes,' and ending
with the words, ' Not wisely but too well.' I have also read in
the issue of the *Freeman's Journal* of Tuesday, 15th August, a
passage commencing ' The conviction of Francis Hynes,' and ending with the words ' Penal servitude will certainly satisfy her.'
    At this period the High Sheriff came into court and sat in one
of the side boxes.
    The Solicitor-General—The first is an extract from the
Freeman's Journal, of August 11 :—
    "Yesterday, at the Commission Court, the first jury trial under
the recent Crimes Act took place. John Connor and three others,
all natives of Kerry, were placed in the dock charged with, on
the 17th March last, at Fahey, in the County of Kerry, having
attacked the house of Mrs. Maybury, the widow of an officer in
the army. Under the ordinary law the men would have been
tried in Kerry, where the alleged offence took place ; but availing
himself of the provision in the Crimes Act, the Attorney-General
removed the case to Dublin, and under the same measure a
special jury was empanelled from a joint county and city panel.
The Crown exercised their right tò challenge on a wholesale scale,
and no less than nineteen persons, some of them among our
most respectable citizens, were ordered to ' stand aside.' All the
facts of the case will be found reported elsewhere. The

prisoners were convicted, but the jury accompanied their finding with a strong recommendation to mercy, and sentence was deferred."

That article standing by itself would have been a most improper, as I respectfully submit, a most improper interference by this public newspaper with the administration of justice in your lordship's court. It is absolutely intolerable, my lord, that it should be permitted to any individual, be he journalist, or whether he belong to any other profession or class in the community, to exercise that right of supervision over the proceedings of your lordship's court which belongs to your lordship, and to your lordship alone. My lord, every person who has even the most elementary acquaintance with the rules of law which govern the criminal procedure of this country, is perfectly aware that the exercise of the right to say "stand by" to a particular juror by the Attorney-General is one which is absolutely unquestionable, so much so that in a case that I have myself been present at a learned and distinguished judge ruled that he would not permit observation or comment upon the exercise of an undoubted and unquestioned right to be made even by the counsel for the prisoner in whose case it was exercised, and to be made even in court—respectfully made to the judge himself who was presiding at the trial, and that for perfectly obvious reasons. My lord, there is no imputation upon a juror in whose case the Attorney-General exercises the right to say " stand by." There are numbers of circumstances which may influence the Attorney-General in taking that course, or those others who represent the Crown, which it is absolutely impossible to have investigated in court, in which the law entrusts to those representing the Crown an absolutely uncontrolled discretion, and in reference to which no inquiry can be possibly permitted, even in court. But the object of the article I have read to your lordship is obvious and plain. It is to discredit the administration of justice, and it is to endeavour to arouse in the minds of those who are attending this court as jurors, a feeling of dissatisfaction against the mode in which business is conducted by your lordship's tribunal, and to interfere with the calm, free and judicial administration of justice in this public court. If comment of this kind were permitted to go on, our jurisprudence would become simply a farce, we would be here for the purpose of doing as we were told by Mr. Edmund Dwyer Gray, of the *Freeman's Journal*, and of course by other journalists in the same way, because, if comment of this kind, while a Commission is actually sitting and whilst jurors are in attendance on the court, is permitted in one newspaper, it must be permitted to all, and there would be an end of the calm and free administration of justice which it is essential should be provided for in our courts.

But that article did not stand alone—it was followed by another on the 12th of August, last Saturday, which is more pronounced ; and I shall read the whole article—

" We are unwilling to credit the rumour that the Crown have resolved that juries exclusively, or almost exclusively, Protestant shall determine in some cases the liberty, in other cases the lives of the prisoners on trial at Green-street. Yet colour is lent to the report by the fact that yesterday, in the capital case, just as on the previous day in the whiteboy case, Catholic gentlemen of admitted respectability and position were ordered to ' stand aside ' when they took the book to be sworn."

Let me pause for a moment to say that such an idea as investigating the religious belief of gentlemen has never entered into the contemplation of those representing the Crown, nor can it or ought it for a moment. I admit that what this journal says as to the respectability of these gentlemen, some of whom we told to " stand by," is undoubted, and the Crown never meant to cast the slightest reproach on them, any more than is conveyed in being challenged by the prisoner.

" To the gentlemen in question no stereotyped ' trade' objection can be, and the inference, therefore, is, that they were shoved aside from their duties as jurors simply because they are Catholics. If this is true, an odious and, it was hoped, obsolete practice has been revived, and the course taken, as unnecessary as it is injudicious, must naturally cause indignation and resentment in Catholic circles. The notion that such men as Edward Lenehan, of Castle-street; William Dennehy, of John-street ; and others whom we could mention, should not be trusted to find a true verdict according to evidence in country cases brought to Dublin for trial, which is the simple and only inference, is offensive in the extreme. The representatives of the Crown would not venture to publicly make such a declaration, yet the names of the gentlemen specified appear in the published list of the rejected. The matter is one that calls for inquiry and explanation. For the present we have only to express our regret that the representatives of the Crown should deem it necessary and expedient to boycott Catholic special jurors of the city and county of Dublin. That this has been done we fear there is no doubt, and we apprehend that no other interpretation of the action of the Crown can be given than that Catholic gentlemen are subjected to the shocking imputation that they are not unprepared to violate the solemn obligation of their oath in cases which are supposed to arise out of political agitation in the country. Would the managers of the Crown prosecutions in Green-street dare openly make such an accusation ?"

Now, my lord, that infinitely transcends in audacity—I use the word advisedly—that which had taken place in the publication of the previous day. What is the obvious and necessary consequence of the publication of an article of that sort ? If it were permitted to go unreproved and unchecked—aye, and unpunished—it would be to stir up class feeling and prejudice amongst the jurors, and render such a thing as a free administration of justice an impossibility. The importance of an article of that kind is that by making these accusations against those representing the Crown, who are merely discharging what they consider to be their duty, in reference to which if they have committed any mistake or impropriety they are responsible under your lordship's jurisdiction—it would be holding up those representing the Crown to the odium of a large portion of the community in which we live, and the endeavour is to fasten upon a large class of jurors the imputation that they are—by those conducting the prosecutions—looked upon as not of faith worthy on oath. Such a statement is absolutely without foundation, but it is made there, and made for a purpose, and probably with an effect—if not checked—of preventing justice being done in courts, of creating class feeling and prejudice in the minds of those very persons on whose impartiality the liberties of prisoners and the rights of the public so largely depend. It seems to me that a publication of that kind, circulating, as undoubtedly it does, amongst the class of jurors in this locality, is one that renders it impossible for the Crown to avoid taking the course they have done in bringing the matter officially under your lordship's notice. These two articles, followed up by some other comments which it will be my duty to bring before your lordship, in the paper of yesterday's date, are bad enough ; but there is another matter which stands upon a somewhat different basis, and which consists of publications which appeared in the paper of Monday. A letter appeared printed in the *Freeman's Journal*, of Monday—not a day had passed (the 13th, of course, was a Sunday)—a letter appeared signed by "William O'Brien." Now, I, personally, my lord, have no knowledge of the writer of the letter nor of who he may be—I have not been even officially informed on that point ; but that letter purports to be a comment upon the conduct of the jury in the Ennis murder case. That was a case in which a verdict of guilty had been brought in by a special jury, guided in reference to the trial by your lordship as judge, and that trial had been completed and ended at the time of this publication. My lord, this letter, of course, bears a signature to it; but whoever the writer of it may be, the publisher of it, whom we know, is the person who is officially responsible, and in reference to whose conduct he must for all purposes be treated precisely as if he had written that article himself. This letter is in these words.

"THE JURY IN THE ENNIS MURDER CASE.

"TO THE EDITOR OF THE 'FREEMAN.'

"*Imperial Hotel, Dublin, Saturday, Aug.* 12.

"DEAR SIR,—I think the public ought to be made aware of the following facts. The jury in the murder case of the Queen *v.* Hynes were last night 'locked up,' as it is termed, for the night at the Imperial Hotel, where I was also staying. I was awakened from sleep shortly after midnight by the sounds of a drunken chorus, succeeded after a time by scuffling, rushing, coarse laughter, and horse-play along the corridor on which my bedroom opens. A number of men, it seemed to me, were falling about the passage in a maudlin state of drunkenness, playing ribald jokes. I listened with patience for a considerable time, when the door of my bedroom was burst open, and a man whom I can identify (for he carried a candle unsteadily in his hand) staggered in, plainly under the influence of drink, hiccuping, 'Hallo, old fellow, all alone?' My answer was of a character that induced him to bolt out of the room in as disordered a manner as he had entered. Having rung the bell, I ascertained that these disorderly persons were jurors in the case of the Queen *v.* Hynes, and that the servants of the hotel had been endeavouring in vain to bring them to a sense of their misconduct. I thought it right to convey to them a warning that the public would hear of their proceedings. The disturbance then ceased. It is fair to add that no more than three or four men appeared to be engaged in the roaring and the tipsy horse-play that followed. I leave the public to judge the loathsomeness of such a scene upon the night when these men held the issues of life and death for a young man in the flower of youth, when they had already heard evidence which, if unbutted, they must have known would send him to a felon's grave. These facts I am ready to support upon oath.

"WILLIAM O'BRIEN."

Now, my lord, presuming—I am assuming in favour of Mr. Gray that that is a genuine letter, and that that' letter he believed to be a genuine communication—that it was received in his office as a genuine and ordinary communication, what was his duty in reference to it? My lord, as a public journalist, I respectfully submit that he ought never to have published such a communication at all. Comment in the newspapers upon the mode in which jurors conduct themselves out of court is a matter which cannot for a moment be permitted. If they commit any misconduct in court, it is for the court to reprove them. If any misconduct is alleged against them, it is for the court to deal with them. The court is the tribunal to which any such complaint ought to be made. But to drag the conduct of jurors before the public after a case is concluded, with the view solely and simply to discredit the verdict at which these jurors have arrived, is an endeavour to tamper with the administration of justice—to defeat it and render it impossible. My lord, the writer of the letter must have known, and if the writer did not know, the publisher of the letter in the paper must have perfectly well known, that it could have no effect if believed in except to raise prejudice in the public mind. So far as the case itself was concerned, the case was concluded and over, and therefore if this case had been merely the publication of a letter of the kind by Mr. Gray in the ordinary course of his business, and as a public journalist, it was a scandalous indecency of a character which could not, I respectfully submit, be permitted to go unpunished—a scandalous indecency, for which he is undoubtedly responsible. But what are the facts of the case? Mr. Gray is not only the publisher of the *Freeman's Journal,* but he is also the High Sheriff of the City of Dublin, and it is so sworn in the affidavit; and if there was anything wrong in the conduct of the jurors after they had left this court, he was the person who was responsible for that himself; and it was his duty, if that matter had been brought before him, to have suppressed and prevented the publication in the newspapers of anything which would be calculated to interfere with the administration of justice, and to have instantly consulted your lordship, or legal advice in the matter, with a view of submitting his own duty or breach of duty to the court with the view of having it tested by the constituted tribunals. Mr. Gray seems to forget that if there is a word of truth in the letter—which I do not for a moment admit—it is a matter which cannot be inquired into. Without admitting there is one shadow of foundation for the statement in the letter, if there was a letter, and he believed it to be true, he has committed a very gross breach of duty in bringing it before the public with a view to raise prejudice against the jurors in that and other cases which may come on for trial here before the court. He was bound, in the discharge of his own duty, to have come to the law under which he was bound to act as a ministerial officer. My lord, the publication does not stop with the letter. There is also a leading article in the same paper, which I will read to your lordship—

" On Saturday, Francis Hynes was found guilty of the murder

of John Doloughty. The circumstances of the case were in
every' sense most lamentable. We cannot think that the
evidence will so far satisfy the public conscience as to induce it
to regard the execution of the capital sentence on Hynes with
equanimity. True, the dying man, when questioned as to the
murder, repeated more than once the words Francy or Francy
Hynes. But, then, the fear of Hynes was long fixed in his
mind, and his wounds were of such a character as to be calculated to unsettle his mind. The mere repetition of a dreaded
name is, under such circumstances, very different from a
detailed story of how the crime was committed. Nothing of
this kind was given, and, on the whole, without desiring in any way
to screen the guilty, we say that it would be safer for the Executive not to rush too hastily to the application of the bloody
penalty in a case in which there certainly is an element of
doubt; and we say that the ends of justice would be better served
if the sentence were commuted. This is an opinion upon the
evidence alone; but what shall we say of the fearful tale given
by Mr. William O'Brien with reference to the conduct of the
jury on the night before they found a verdict which was to
bring Hynes to a dishonoured grave? It is fearful; it is
horrible; it makes one shudder. In what state of mind can
these men have been, when, a few hours after the proceedings
described, they were called upon to decide whether a fellow-
creature was to live or die? Can the Executive refuse to take
cognizance of Mr. O'Brien's proffered evidence? Can they
refuse to act upon it if proved to be true? Knowing Mr.
O'Brien as we do, we place the most absolute confidence in
every word he says. But let the Executive test his veracity. If
it remain unimpeached, then we say that his disclosures are
such as to make us blush for our common humanity. We have
heard of men hanging that jurymen may dine; but what of a
man hanging because jurymen have dined—not wisely but too
well?"

My lord, I was not present at any portion of the trial. I
have, however, made myself acquainted with the proceedings as
they occurred in court, and your lordship, as presiding judge,
of course, was present during every moment of the trial, and I
think I may state that which is in the knowledge of every person
who was present in court, and which I have no reason whatever
for a moment to doubt, that a more perfectly calm, careful,
honest investigation than was given to the case by the jury who
tried it it would be impossible to conceive. Their conduct was
exemplary in the extreme from the commencement to the conclusion of the case, and that as to the appearance of misconduct
or of anything which would entitle the writer of any article in

morals much less in law to hold them up to the odium and execration of the community in which they live, never could be dreamt of. In the first part of the article we have a discussion of the case, and the writer of that article, whoever he may be— of course I don't know; it is an anonymòus article ; I don't know who the writer may be—but he thinks that, writing in Prince's-street, he is constituting himself a court of appeal from your lordship and from the jury who heard the case; and he is to pronounce, in the name of justice, that the proceedings— at a single moment of which he probably was not present— were all wrong ; that everybody who took part in the proceedings was guilty of a monstrous miscónduct, but that he alone is an absolutely infallible judge, and perfectly competent to sit as a court of appeal over the proceedings of judge and jury. But as regards the latter portion, in which comment is made upon the letter of Mr. William O'Brien, it certainly appears to me that it transcends in the qualities I have already referred to, in audacity, the previoùs part of the article. The jurors who attend at this court have cast upon them by law duties of the utmost gravity. There never was a time in the history of the law when the discharge of their duties uninfluenced by terror or fear was more vitally essential. That is the time in which this anonymous writer—for whose every word Mr. Gray is just as responsible as if he had written them himself—selects for the purpose of pilloring the jurors in reference to the charge of misconduct which is continued down to the very time the verdict was given, because the meaning is, that sentence of death was pronounced upon the man because the jury were intoxicated at the time. That was followed by a long correspondence in the same paper of yesterday. The first portion of the article is headed, " Conviction of Francis Hynes."

Judge Lawson—What is the date of this ?

The Solicitor General—Tuesday, August 15th, the *Freeman's Journal*. It is all under the one heading. The first portion I need not read ; it is merely a report of the application made yesterday by the jury. Then it goes on—

" TO THE EDITOR OF THE ' FREEMAN.'

" *Imperial Hotel, Monday Night.*

" DEAR SIR—As my accusátion against certain jurors in the case of the Queen *v.* Hynes is to form the subject of judicial inquiry, I shall only say in reference to Mr. Barrett's statement in the Commission Court to-day, that further evidence which has now come to my knowledge makes me more anxious than ever to court the fullest investigation as to the truth of my charge.

"Your faithful servant,

"WILLIAM O'BRIEN."

That is a reiteration of the charge already published by the High Sheriff on the officers of this court.

"The following letter has been furnished to us by telegraph for publication by Mr. Edward Finucane, Ennis :—

"'TO THE EDITOR OF THE "FREEMAN."

"'In reference to Mr. Justice Lawson's comment on cross-examination of young Doloughty in the Clare murder case, where, relative to conversation of his with an Ennis shopkeeper, his lordship said it showed the lengths people interested in defeating the ends of justice will go—I am the shopkeeper referred to, and am as well known to be incapable of acting such a part as the judge who decided according to law that a cool and uninvited statement made to me by the boy was inadmissible, as even my servant also heard his distinct statement, in reply to my remark deploring the murder of his father, and referring to the arrest of Hynes, that as nothing will be done to him, because whoever would do it he would say it was Francy Hynes. I did not volunteer to give evidence, but feel surprised the law, of which Judge Lawson is the mouthpiece, refused to hear facts which no juryman could doubt, and which would enable them to judge the state of mind the murdered man was in even before the awful occurrence.' "

The prisoner on the occasion was represented by able counsel, who knew how to conduct his case, and if there had been any misconduct or omission on the part of the jury or your lordship in reference to the admission of evidence or not attaching proper weight to it, it was for them to comment on it, and not obscure scribblers in newspapers.

Judge Lawson—I can only say that The MacDermot, who conducted the case, did not press this evidence, it was so manifestly inadmissible.

The Solicitor General—He was too much of a lawyer.

Judge Lawson—Things have come to a nice pass when a man of this kind will write about a judge.

The Solicitor-General—There is another letter :—

"TO THE EDITOR OF THE 'FREEMAN.'

"6 *Upper Ormond Quay, Aug.* 14.

"DEAR SIR—As the solicitor who was engaged in instructing counsel and otherwise acting in the defence of the prisoner, I

❀

beg to lay before your readers and the public a short statement of some facts that marked the course of procedure on this tria in a way that struck me as very inconsistent with what should be calculated to inspire faith and confidence in the administration of the laws of this or any other country."

My lord, that is plain speaking—what occurred is calculated, that is the meaning of it, to deprive the proceedings in courts of faith or confidence in the administration of the law, and that is the object for which it is published. It is to bring the administration of the law into contempt and render the execution of the law impossible.

" The sheriffs of the county and city of Dublin returned each a special panel of 100 men to try the several cases which would be sent up from the provinces to the present commission. For the purposes of the present case I will assume that each of these two panels was chosen with perfect fairness by the respective sheriffs of the county and city. I know the sheriff of the city to be an honourable man. At this moment I do not know the name of the sheriff of the county, but I assume him also to be an Irish gentleman, and perfectly honourable— for why should any man of that rank be otherwise in the discharge of so serious a public duty ? "

When he is writing to Mr. Edmund Dwyer Gray, the sheriff of the city, he assumes no person in his position will be guilty of any breach of public duty, and I venture to say in returning a jury there is no fault to be attached to Mr. Gray ; he was acting under a statute and did his duty under it. I don't for a moment say it was written by a solicitor; there is no application against him, but it is printed by Mr. Gray as if it were. Mr. Gray publishes that compliment to himself ; but what does he say about the jurors who are in a public position at least as important, and what does he say about the judge ?—

" However, when the jury came to be selected in open court, in the presence of the Attorney-General and the other counsel engaged in the prosecution for the Crown, what took place ? The gentleman acting as solicitor for the Crown, as it appears he had a legal right to do, in exercise of the powers with which he is vested by the laws as at present constituted, ordered every gentleman of the Roman Catholic persuasion or of Liberal principles in politics to stand aside, as if unworthy to serve on that jury. I have been upwards of thirty years engaged in my profession, and must say that I was never more amazed than at this what I consider extreme step on the part of those acting for the Crown towards a young person who was brought far away from his home, and before jurors to whom he or his antecedents were wholly unknown, but who were still the persons called upon to pronounce on his guilt or innocence. Whilst the jury were being empanelled I felt it my duty to challenge eleven out of the forty-nine who were called and answered, but what was my astonishment to find the Crown ordered not less than twenty-six of those specially summoned jurors to stand aside as if unfit to sit in judgment as jurors on the case, and particularly when I was constrained to observe that amongst the persons so included were also those who happened to be called who professed the religious or political principles to which I have before referred.

"JOHN FROST."

He admits he exercised his rights of challenge, which is a very different right to saying "stand aside." When a juror is challenged he cannot absolutely be called again on that case ; "stand by" passes the juror over, but does not prevent him serving if there is a defect of jurors. What is the impression to be left on the minds of these gentlemen who are told to stand aside? It is that the Crown is partisan and actuated by feelings hostile to those jurors who in the exercise of their discretion for many reasons, some of them reasons in which the jurors would themselves most perfectly acquiesce, have been passed over. My lord, there is only one other letter :—

"14th August.

"DEAR SIR,—Would it not be advisable, considering all the circumstances of this unfortunate man's case, that a memorial should be prepared for signature to be presented to the Lord Lieutenant, praying a remission of the capital punishment; and I feel certain that the jury will lead the way. The Crown desires no victim, only that justice may be vindicated, and penal servitude will certainly satisfy her.

"SPES.
"I enclose my name, &c."

Of course I only include that as being portion of the publication, of that day. Now, my lord, the principles on which this court acts in reference to publications in the public press are perfectly clear, and perfectly settled, and do not admit of question. It would be pedantry to be citing authorities to your lordship. Any publication in the public press which is calculated in the mind of the presiding judge to interfere with the free exercise of the duty of a court and the administration of justice is a contempt of court. It is true that the comment in reference to the jury in Hynes' case was after the trial had concluded, and if it were only in reference to that trial there would be something to be said as to whether that was a contempt of court, but the court had not concluded its business. These same gentlemen who took part in the trial are liable to serve—I presume some of them did serve in subsequent cases—your lordship is still bound to remain until the business of the Commission has closed; and an attack upon the jury in that particular case cannot for a moment be treated as if it were merely comment upon a particular case if it is obvious that the publication was not confined to that case but must extend to the entire administration of justice. Is Mr. Gray responsible for the publication of these articles, or is he not? The affidavit from which I have read makes exhibits of the papers and says—

"I say the said *Freeman's Journal*——

The High Sheriff—Perhaps I may save the Solicitor-General trouble by saying I acknowledge my responsibility.

The Solicitor-General—The affidavit says —" Is printed and published in the city of Dublin, and circulates largely in the county and city of Dublin, and amongst the class of persons who are upon the jury panels respectively, and I say the said publication in my opinion is calculated to interfere with the due administration of justice and the free and impartial discharge of their duties by the jurors in the Commission Court; and I am advised and submit that the publication of these articles are a contempt of this court. I say that Mr. Edmund Dwyer Gray, who is at present the High Sheriff of the city of Dublin, is the sole proprietor of the *Freeman's Journal*, upon each copy of which his name appears as publisher." Then he referred to the copies of the paper. I don't press this application merely upon the ground of an attempt to interfere with the administration of justice so far as the jurors who have already served—I rest it with reference to the jurors of the entire of this Commission. The object of these articles is to stir up partizanship, which will render a fair trial impossible. I also press it in reference to comments upon the conduct of the presiding judge, though I know your lordship will be most unwilling to entertain it, but which in the discharge of your duty sitting here you must. I shall wait to hear what apology or explanation will be offered. I don't suppose Mr. Gray nor did Mr. Pigott in the case in which he was punished—the court cannot deal with; the question of who is the precise scribe who wrote the article. If you find the proprietor of a newspaper receiving the profits of such comment, he is absolutely responsible, and the court cannot enter into any explanation of whether he did or did not write or know of the publication of these articles. It will be open to Mr. Gray or his counsel to satisfy your lordship, if he can, that these documents are not of the character I have described. It will be open for him to show that they are not inconsistent with the calm discharge of their duty by the tribunal in reference to whom they were published. If that cannot be done, and if it be impossible to convey any other idea but that these documents are calculated to tamper with the free administration of justice,

D

I apprehend your lordship will have no alternative but to deal
with such publication as a very gross and dangerous contempt
of court, and deal with it in such a manner as your lordship
thinks fit.

The High Sheriff—In reference to this application, I wish in
the first instance to state that through the courtesy of Mr.
Morphy, the Crown Solicitor, I was handed last evening,
at rather a late hour, just when I was leaving my house,
a document conveying a notice to me that at 11 o'clock
this morning a motion would be made to your lordship,
on behalf of her Majesty's Attorney-General for Ireland,
that I should be forthwith committed to prison for contempt of court. As I have stated to your lordship, it was at
a late hour last evening that I received this notice, and I have
not had time since sufficient to instruct counsel or to consult
a solicitor, and I must, therefore, throw myself somewhat on
your lordship's consideration in making such statements as I
may think it necessary to make on the subject of this application. I am not aware of the course of procedure customary in
cases of this kind. I certainly was under the impression that
the usual form of such an application was that the person
accused should be required to attend before the court to show
cause—that the usual course was that of an *ex parte* application
to fix a day when the case should be heard and the accused
person permitted to come before the court and show cause
against the application, or adopt such course as he or his
counsel might deem advisable.

Judge Lawson—You are the High Sheriff, and you are bound
to be always in attendance on the court.

The High Sheriff—Even so, my lord, my being bound as
High Sheriff to be present in your lordship's court would not
furnish me with the formal notice to which I have referred.
My lord, as I say, I was under the impression that the course I
have pointed out was the regular form of procedure in such
application, as it, I certainly think, is the usual course which
has been adopted in similar cases. I was only saying that the
usual form of procedure was not that I should be sentenced first
and tried afterwards, as the Solicitor-General apparently
proposes. Now, my lord, there is one point perfectly
clear. I do not think it will require many words to convince
your lordship that in the articles and letters which appeared in
the *Freeman's Journal*, of which newspaper I acknowledge that I
am the proprietor, and for everything appearing in which I am,
of course, responsible—that no personal disrespect whatever
either to your lordship or your lordship's court was intended to
be conveyed.

Judge Lawson—I would not entertain any application what-ever founded on personal disrespect to myself. I would consider it quite unworthy of dealing with.

The High-Sheriff—I am sure your lordship would not, and that you do not, attribute any such motive or intention ; but at the same time I desire emphatically to disclaim on the part of all concerned, and most emphatically on my own part, any suggestion of the kind. As a matter of fact, I do not think the articles bear that construction ; but, lest any person should think they do, I think it my duty to say none such was intended. It is a question whether there is technical contempt to the court, certainly not to your lordship. Now, my lord, I wish to say a word with regard to the observations made by the Solicitor-General as to the peculiar and anomalous position which I occupy, owing to the fact of my being High Sheriff, as well as proprietor and conductor of the newspaper in which the articles appeared, which have been impugned. The Solicitor-General seems to be under the impression that in that dual capacity it was my duty to suppress the publication in the *Freeman's Journal* of any articles or communications in reference to the trials in this court. I beg to state that when I accepted the office of High Sheriff of the city I was under the impression that my acceptance of that position would in no way interfere with the honest discharge of my duties as a public journalist, and I can only say that my view as to those duties differs very widely indeed from that which has been stated by the Solicitor-General, and if he is right I can only ask the Crown to relieve me from the discharge of those duties for the discharge of duties which I consider much more important. In my opinion it is the duty of a public journalist to comment freely and fearlessly upon the conduct of public tribunals, and upon the mode in which justice is administered in this country. Now, the charges which the Solicitor-General has made against the *Free-man's Journal* are of a two-fold character. One charge, or one set of charges, has reference to the imputations which he alleges have been made by those "scribblers"—that being the language he has thought fit to use with reference to the writers in the public Press—to the effect that we charged the representatives of the Crown with unduly exercising their right of challenge, and exercising it in such a manner as to prejudice the fair trial of the accused. Now, the Solicitor-General appears exceedingly anxious to dissociate the representatives of the Crown from any imputa-tion of that character. Any person listening to the long and able speech he made would be under the impression—did he not know the facts—that jury-packing was quite an unknown thing in the history of the administration of the law in Ireland. That may be the view of the Solicitor-General ; but it certainly is not the general impression of the people of this country, and it is not mine. I need not point out to your lordship that whether those charges be true or false, that it is in point of fact quite as possibly to pack a jury by exclusion as it is by inclusion, and that if out of an enormous number of jurymen the Crown exercise to an undue extent its rights of setting aside, it may secure a jury who will to a moral certainty find a verdict in accordance with its view. Now, I put that merely as a matter of possibility. I am not saying that it has been done at this Commission—whether it has or not remains to be seen—but as a matter of fact I assert that a jury can be packed by the Crown by a system of exclusion quite as effectually as by a system of inclusion. The real question, I take it, is whether that charge is true or not. The Solicitor-General seems to think that it is out of your lordship's province to inquire into the matter. If it is, I suppose it will go by default and the only question will be the amount of punishment, or what term of imprisonment your lordship should mete out to me. But the question, it seems to me, is whether the statement was true or not. Was the right of exclusion exercised to an undue extent by the Crown ? Were Catholics ordered to stand aside because they were Catholics? Were Liberals directed to stand by because they were Liberals ? Were jurors of a certain complexion selected by the Crown by means of that system of exclusion ? Now I am not in a position to go into that question to-day, and on that point I would ask your lordship, if you can see your way to it, to grant some adjournment of the case in order that the action of the Crown in connection with the selection or exclusion of jurors may be more carefully investigated, and if it shall be found that the statements made in the *Freeman's Journal* in that regard were unfounded, I may offer to the representatives of the Crown and your lordship such apology and render such reparation as your lordship shall deem necessary. But if, on the other hand, I find on inquiry that the charges are to my mind well founded, I shall ask permission to lay before you, either by affidavit or in such other way as may be proper, such evidence as I may be able to procure in support of the statements that have been made.

I now come to what I regard as a much more serious matter— the letter of Mr. William O'Brien and the comments of the *Freeman's Journal* thereon. Now, I am not only responsible as proprietor of the *Freeman's Journal* for the publication of that letter, but I have no hesitation in avowing that I am personally responsible for it, and also for the comments which appeared upon it, inasmuch as I knew of its insertion, and it was I myself that wrote the article which the Solicitor-General has characterised in such emphatic language. The Solicitor-General says that he knows nothing of Mr. William O'Brien, the writer of that letter. But suffice it to say—I don't want to occupy unduly your lordship's time—that Mr. O'Brien is sufficiently well-known in this city to have enabled the Solicitor-General to have ascertained his character by inquiry. Suffice it to say, I know Mr. William O'Brien, and that I published the letter because I knew it was a *bona fide* letter, written by a gentleman residing in the hotel—a gentleman whose friendship I enjoy— of whom I have intimate personal knowledge, and whom I believe to be absolutely incapable of stating anything which was not true. Now, so far from the facts as stated by Mr. O'Brien being exaggerated——

Judge Lawson interrupted—You had better not enter into that; that is a matter that is stated on the hearsay of a waiter. I cannot enter into it. As has been already stated by the Solicitor-General, you, as High Sheriff, had the custody of those jurors, and it was your duty to see that they conducted them- selves in a proper and becoming manner. I must assume that you did your duty, and I decline to enter into any such inquiry.

The High Sheriff—My lord, I think that portion of the state- ment of the Solicitor-General was the only thing of which I have personal reason to complain. He stated that I, as an officer of the court, was responsible for the way in which the jury behaved. Now, of course the High Sheriff nominally has custody of the jurors, but it is well-known, and the Solicitor- General must have been aware, that, though the High Sheriff is nominally responsible, the Sub-Sheriff and his officers do the entire work.

Judge Lawson—That does not render the High Sheriff less responsible. I hold you as High Sheriff to be responsible for everything.

The High Sheriff—What I was complaining of was the state- ment made by the Solicitor-General, which was calculated to convey a false impression upon those who were not aware of the facts. I believe the actual course is that a number of persons are sworn in by the court itself as special constables to take charge of the jury, and those individuals are in public court sworn in to take charge of the jury; and while I do not deny the nominal responsibility of the High Sheriff, I respectfully say the real responsibility rests upon those persons who are selected by the court with reference to their fitness, and sworn for the purpose of discharging the duty.

Judge Lawson again interrupted—That is an entire mistake. The jurors are delivered into the custody of the High Sheriff, and the bailiffs who are sworn are under the authority of the Sheriff to assist him in taking charge of the jury.

The High Sheriff—Then, my lord, the Attorney-General may have something by-and-by to say with regard to my conduct as Sheriff if it be shown that those jurors were, owing to the negligence of my subordinates, permitted to misconduct themselves. The Solicitor-General says that this is not a question which can be investigated, but in my judgment it is a question whether as a public journalist having been informed that these jurors had misconducted themselves in the hotel, and being informed, as I subsequently have been, that they had been drinking in the public billiard-room of the hotel in company with——

Judge Lawson again interrupted—You had better not make any statements of that character. They will not at all assist your case—unwise statements.

The High Sheriff—Well, my lord, I make this statement. I shall not follow them up further.

Judge Lawson—I may state that from the statement of the foreman, a most respectable gentleman, I believe them to be perfectly destitute of truth.

The High Sheriff—I am informed that those jurors · were drinking that night in the public billiard-room of the hotel.

Judge Lawson—I must request you not to repeat that statement.

Mr. Barrett (foreman)—The jury court every investigation.

Mr. William O'Brien—My lord, I do not know whether, as the writer of the letter, you will listen to a statement from me——

Judge Lawson—I beg your pardon, sir. Sit down, sir. I am not going to investigate the matter. I have no power to do so. If an action for libel were brought against this man, whoever he is, who wrote that letter, of course the truth or falsehood of the statement might possibly appear ; but in the present case, Mr. High Sheriff, the charge against you is that you committed a contempt of court by the publication of these statements.

The High Sheriff—My lord, I respectfully submit the question is whether I, as a public journalist, having, as I thought, sufficient reason to believe that the statements were true, acted rightly in publishing them or not. The trial was over at the time ; the jury had been discharged, and I certainly was under the impression—of course I may have been wrong—I do not profess to understand the law—but I have always been of opinion that it was the right, and in certain cases the duty, of a public journalist to comment on trials of this kind after they had been concluded, and if it were shown that anything of an irregular or an improper character had taken place, that it was one of the functions of the public Press to bring it before the public. The Solicitor-General says that so long as the Commission lasts we are not justified in making comments of this kind. Now I will put a hypothetical case. This man Francis Hynes is to be hanged in three weeks. Suppose the Commission last for four weeks, it would be, according to the Solicitor General, our duty to refrain from bringing this matter before the public till a week after the man was hanged! That may be law, but it does not appear to me to be common sense. I consider that if those facts were true—I do not propose to discuss them further, as your lordship says I am not to do so—the statements in the *Freeman's Journal*, so far from involving any suggestion of interference with the administration of justice in this or any other court, a suggestion which I utterly disclaim and repudiate—I say, so far from doing anything of the kind, that we were materially assisting the administration of justice by bringing before the public, as well as before the court and before your lordship, any facts which might affect the regularity of the proceedings in this court. As owing to the circumstances I have stated, I am here without any professional assistance, I would ask your lordship to adjourn this case for such time as you may deem fit in order to afford me an opportunity of procuring professional assistance, with the view of putting in such form as I may be advised the facts which I have indicated in my statement. I repeat that if I find that we have stated anything untrue, I am ready to apologise in the fullest possible manner to the court. As I said to your lordship, there was no kind of idea in my mind or, I am sure, in the minds of the conductors of the *Freeman's Journal*, to be guilty of any kind of disrespect or contempt of court. What we did we did honestly, believing we were discharging our public duty, and believing that duty was as important in its way, perhaps, as the duty discharged by the Solicitor-General. If your lordship will permit it, the writer of the letter is in court and ready to testify to his knowledge of the facts ; and if those facts be as stated, I say that the language of the leading article—" They were horrible and fearful, and calculated to make one shudder and blush for our common humanity" —was not stronger under the circumstances than the facts would justify. I would ask your lordship under the circumstance to give me an opportunity of procuring professional assistance, as it is not very pleasant to go to prison, as has been proposed by the Solicitor-General, and I wish to be enabled to place some facts before your lordship which may induce you to take a more lenient view of the matter.

Mr. William O'Brien—My lord, in justice to Mr. Gray will you permit me to say a word ?

Judge Lawson—I told you not to speak before ! Police, remove that man.

Mr. O'Brien—My lord, I am the writer of that letter, and I am ready to justify every word that I have written.

Judge Lawson—Remove that person. If you dare to disturb the court any more I will put you in the dock.

Mr. O'Brien—Very well, my lord. [Mr. O'Brien then left the court.]

The Solicitor-General—I would acquiesce in the application for an adjournment if Mr. Gray had made the application in the first instance, but as representing the Crown, Mr. Gray having made a very full statement, I cannot consent now to an adjournment.

Judge Lawson—In my opinion there is no ground for adjournment in this case whatever, and the only two matters that can be in controversy according to law are—first, is Mr. Gray responsible for the publication of these articles; he admits it himself, and it has been proved ; and, secondly, which is a matter for me, in writing the articles and all the circumstances, are they articles that constitute contempt of court? In other words, do they tend to interfere with the administration of justice ? Are they calculated to interfere, and were they intended so to interfere ? Now, I have had considerable experience in applications of this kind. I remember in one case in Belfast, where I presided at a very important Commission there, on the very second day on which the Commission sat there, a journalist in that city thought proper to write articles of this kind reflecting upon the trial of a case that was then over, and reflecting upon the mode in which the jurors were summoned. The editor of that paper was brought before me by the proper authorities—those representing the Crown at the time. He was represented by a very able gentleman, Mr. Butt, and the matter was brought forward by him, and I felt it my duty to sentence the editor to fine and imprisonment. The result was, those comments ceased, for I was perfectly satisfied that unless I interfered in that way those comments would have been continued, and would have rendered it quite impossible that the operations of the Commission could have been carried on with that freedom and that absence of fear and apprehension which is necessary in conducting the administration of justice. In my opinion each and every of these articles constitute a grievous contempt of court. I think the earlier ones, containing those atrocious allegations about the exclusion of Catholics from the jury, are specially a contempt of court, and they are written for one purpose, and one purpose only; namely, to excite in the mind of gentlemen of this persuasion attending on this jury panel an idea that they are ostracised or unfairly dealt with, and the intention is that when any Catholics are called on a subsequent jury there should be an impression left on their mind which would prevent them, and interfere with a due and proper discharge of the administration of justice. In my opinion jurors, of all persons in the community, require to be protected in the discharge of their duty. As to judges, that is not much matter; they are probably able to protect themselves, but jurors come here and act without fee or reward; they undertake, not voluntarily, but compulsorily, most arduous duties. They have upon these occasions been summoned according to law by the very publisher and writer of these articles, and in obedience to that summons they come here and attend, and are they to be subjected to intimidation of this kind, and denunciations—for I can call it nothing else—that is, the denunciations of these gentlemen who discharged their duty so well in that case of Hynes—of the clearest kind, alleging that they were totally unfit for the discharge of their duty. I must say, as the judge presiding at that trial, I never saw a jury exhibit more intelligence or care to the evidence, and I think one of the strongest proofs of that was that I myself on the evening when the case was tried, in considering painfully and carefully over the case, one point struck me which had not been developed or alluded to in the evidence, and I had a great wish to have that point elucidated. The very first thing that occurred in the morning when the jury appeared in the box was that one of them desired to be satisfied on that point, showing that they themselves had gone through the same mental process as I had gone through, and that this had struck them as an important point. Therefore, I reject altogether the idea that the gentlemen composing that panel were capable of the atrocious conduct imputed to them. I believe it to be a thorough invention, and treat it as such. There is a letter and leading article. I would not allude to this, but what is the position of a jury discharging their duty in this court—what is the position of those twelve jurors denounced and held up to public execration in the *Freeman's Journal?* We know that jurors have lost their lives in this country, and in one remarkable instance—that of Mr. Herbert in the County Kerry, who lost his life for discharging his duties as a juror; and I, as a public judge, am to sit here and tolerate this conduct. I should be unworthy of the position I hold if I did not mark these proceedings in the strongest manner with a sense of my disapproval, and so far as I can endeavour to protect juries. I see perfectly well that the design of all those articles is one—it was to endeavour to destroy in the public mind the moral effect of these convictions. That was the object and nothing else, and to interfere with the trial of subsequent prisoners, and prevent juries from bringing to the discharge of their duties that free, that unfettered judgment, which every man should have when he comes to discharge his duty. I think the position of Mr. Gray greatly aggravates his offence. I think he owes a duty to the court which he has most seriously neglected. If there were any imputation against these gentlemen, there was a mode of putting it in a proper train for inquiry If there is an imputation against the Crown for having packed a jury after the Commission is over, that may be inquired into in the proper place, but during the pendency of the Commission to attack the Crown for packing juries, and juries for acting improperly on insufficient evidence, and to attack the judge for rejecting evidence which he onght to have admitted, that is a state of things which cannot be tolerated, and I, therefore, feel bound in the exercise of the undoubted discretion I have, to sentence Mr. Edmund Dwyer Gray both to imprisonment and fine. And accordingly the sentence of the court is, that it appears on the application of the Solicitor-General and this affidavit that these articles constitute a contempt of court, and I order that Mr. Edmund Dwyer Gray be imprisoned for three calendar months, and that he be fined £500, and at the termination of the three months he give security, himself in £5,000 and two securities in £2,500 each, to be of good behaviour and keep the peace towards her Majesty the Queen and all her subjects ; and in default of his giving security, he be further imprisoned for three months. And I now wish it to be understood that if any other newspapers write articles of a similar character as long as this Commission is sitting and they are brought before me in the same way, I shall deal with them with quite as much severity as I have dealt with Mr. Gray. Let the Coroner now take him into custody.

Mr. Gray asked for a short time to dispose of some private affairs.

Judge Lawson—In prison you will have time enough to dispose of your private affairs, and I shall not deal with you differently from any other person.

The City Coroner (Dr. Whyte)—My lord, am I to understand that I am the officer to carry out your lordship's order to commit the High Sheriff to prison ?

Judge Lawson—Certainly. You, as Coroner, are the proper officer.

Dr. Whyte—My lord, how am I to carry out such an order as that ? I have no precedent for it. It is wholly unprecedented.

Judge Lawson—You must carry out the order the court has made, or you must take the consequences.

Dr. Whyte—Of course, I will carry out your lordship's order, but I have no precedent to guide me.

Judge Lawson—Do you mean, Mr. Coroner, to discharge your duty or not ?

Dr. Whyte—Certainly, my lord, if I am bound to do so.

Judge Lawson—You are bound to do so, sir ; and if you don't do it at once I will call on the Sheriff of the County of Dublin to do it.

Dr. Whyte—My lord, you have not named to what prison the High Sheriff is to be committed.

At this observation his lordship paused for a moment, and then said—Mr. Murphy, what is the legal prison ?

Mr. Murphy, Q.C., handed up to the bench a copy of the Act of Parliament.

Mr. Ormsby (the Sub-Sheriff)—Richmond prison, my lord—Richmond is the prison.

Judge Lawson—Yes, Richmond prison.

Dr. Whyte—Am I personally to convey the High Sheriff to the prison, my lord ?

Judge Lawson—Certainly. You shall have any assistance you require in doing so.

Mr. Gray was then removed from court in the custody of the Coroner.

————

I hereby certify the foregoing is a *verbatim* report of the proceedings in this case, at Green-street, on August 16th, 1882, reported by me in shorthand.

CHARLES RYAN,

Shorthand Writer.

September 5th, 1882.

——:o:——

MR. GRAY'S CONDUCT AS HIGH SHERIFF.

——:o:——

The following refer to Mr. Gray's conduct as High Sheriff:—

" To His Excellency Earl Spencer, K.G., Lord Lieutenant, &c.,
DUBLIN CASTLE.

" Your Excellency—I understand that it is your Excellency's intention
to order an inquiry into certain charges against the jury in the case of the
Queen against Hynes, made in a letter in the *Freeman's Journal* of the 14th
inst.

" For the publication of that letter, and asking an inquiry into these
charges, I am now in prison.

" Your Attorney-General in the House of Commons, your Solicitor-General
in public court, the Judge on the Bench, and a section of the public Press,
have all sought to fix upon me, personally and individually, as High Sheriff,
the responsibility of the custody of the jury in that case.

" The inquiry must necessarily involve the investigation of this charge
against me—a charge which, if substantiated, might entail heavy penalties
upon me. I therefore claim, as a matter of justice, to be present at that
inquiry, to be represented, if I so desire, by counsel ; to have the right to
examine and cross-examine witnesses, if necessary ; and to get adequate
notice of the time of holding same.

" Of course I am quite willing to attend the inquiry—which I presume will be
public and upon oath—in the custody of your jailers.

" If any technical legal difficulty exists as to my leaving the jail for that purpose, then I respectfully submit that justice requires that the inquiry shall be
held within the precincts of this prison, so as to admit of my presence thereat.

I have the honour to be,

Your Excellency's obedient servant,

" (Signed),   E. Dwyer Gray,
" High Sheriff, Dublin City,
" M.P. Carlow County.

" Richmond Bridewell Jail,
"August 21st, 1882."

"Dublin Castle,
"21st *August*, 1882.

" Sir—I am directed by the Lord Lieutenant to inform you that his Excellency has no intention of holding any public inquiry into the matters mentioned in your letter of yesterday's date.

" His Excellency has just received certain affidavits respecting the conduct of the jury in the case of the Queen v. Hynes.

" His Excellency has not yet been able to peruse these affidavits, but he will at once examine into the statements contained in them, with the view of satisfying himself whether there are any sufficient grounds for interfering with the ordinary course of the law in that case.

" I am, Sir,

" Your obedient servant,

" R. G. C. HAMILTON.

"E. D. GRAY, ESQ., M.P.,
" High Sheriff of the City of Dublin."

MR. GRAY'S ABSENCE WAS SANCTIONED BY THE JUDGE

" Richmond Bridewell Jail,
August 20th, 1882.

' MY LORD—Under the circumstances which have since arisen I hope you will consider that I am entitled to ask of you, as I now do, a formal acknowledgment of my letter addressed to you immediately before the opening of the present Commission, in which I informed you of my contemplated absence from your Court, and requested you not to attribute it to want of respect for your Lordship or the Court.

" I have the honour to be

" Your obedient servant,

" E. DWYER GRAY,

" High Sheriff, Dublin City.

" THE RIGHT HON. MR. JUSTICE LAWSON,
"27 Upper Fitzwilliam Street."

"Green Street,
"21st *August*, 1882.

" SIR—In reply to your letter of yesterday, I beg to say that I did receive a letter from you, prior to the opening of the Commission, in which you stated that your Parliamentary duties would compel your absence from the Commission, and trusting that I would not attribute it to any want of respect.

"It was not from any want of courtesy that I did not reply to that letter, but I considered that it did not require any answer, as the excuse for your absence was quite sufficient, and you did not ask for, nor did you require any formal leave of absence from me.

"I have the honour to be, Sir,

"Your obedient servant,

"JAMES A. LAWSON.

" E. D. GRAY, ESQ.,
    " High Sheriff."

HOW THE HOTEL WAS SELECTED.'

"Richmond Jail,

" Dublin, 18th September, 1882.

" DEAR SIR—My attention has just been called to the following statement from a correspondent of the Whitehall Review, and published in the paper of the 14th instant with reference to my imprisonment:—

. "'Now as to Mr. Gray, from the fact of his being High Sheriff, the jury in the Hynes murder case were in his charge, and much against their openly expressed wish, they were brought to an hotel patronized by the Land League. A corridor was set apart for them to sleep in, but, strange to say, one of the rooms in the said corridor was occupied by a person closely connected with one of the most inflammatory Land League papers in existence. Next we have a letter stating that the jury were drunk, and an article stating that jurors were excluded because they were Roman Catholics. Both appeared in the Freeman's Journal: and both were equally false. The object sought is plain enough to the common sense of any one.'

"This contains in specific terms a charge which has more than once been suggested in the London and Dublin Press. As I was in London on the night in.question and for days previous and did not return until after the jury were discharged, I knew nothing whatever about your arrangements for providing for them. I think it therefore right to ask you to state to me officially all the circumstances in connection with the selection of the particular hotel where the jury slept on the night of the 12th August, although I am personally aware that the Imperial Hotel is one of the most respectable in Dublin.

" Yours faithfully,

" E. DWYER GRAY, High Sheriff.

" JAMES CAMPBELL, Sub-Sheriff,
    " 8 Inns' Quay."

" 8 Inns' Quay,

" Dublin, 20th September, 1882.

"DEAR SIR—In reply to your letter of the 18th inst., requesting me to state the circumstances in connection with the selection of the Imperial Hotel for the accommodation of the jury on the night of the 11th of August last, I beg to say that about 12 o'clock on said 11th August, foreseeing that the case of the Queen v. Hynes, then at trial, would probably not conclude that day, I proceeded to the European Hotel, the nearest to and in close proximity with the Court-house, Green-street, where I had on previous occasions provided for jurors in similar circumstances to their entire contentment, and made arrangements with the proprietor to accommodate the jury in case it became necessary. However, some of the jurors objected to being taken there, and named various other hotels, which, they said, were preferable. At about four o'clock, knowing that the Dublin hotels were very much crowded, owing to the approaching opening of the Exhibition and the unveiling of the O'Connell Statue, and fearing it might be difficult if deferred, to provide for so many persons, I proceeded to the Imperial Hotel, where on two previous occasions I had lodged juries during trials; and, although at first refused, owing to the crowded state of the house, I, with some difficulty, induced the manager to receive the jury. The satisfactory manner in which the juries in my charge had been treated there on the former occasions referred to, and the objection of some of the jurors to the European, were my only reasons for selecting that establishment: one of the most respectable in the city.

"I am, dear Sir,

"Very truly yours,

"JAMES CAMPBELL.

"E. DWYER GRAY, ESQ., M.P.,
    "High Sheriff."

THE BLACK VAN.

"Richmond Prison,
    "*Dublin, 4th September, 1882.*

"DEAR SIR—I will be extremely obliged if you would let me know in writing, whether it is or is not a fact, that without solicitation from you the authorities of Dublin Castle, through one of their police inspectors, Mr. Ward, as I have been informed, offered to you a black van in which to convey me from Green-street Court-house to this prison on the 16th August.

"Yours faithfully,

"(Signed),

"E. DWYER GRAY.

"DR. N. C. WHYTE,
    "Ardgowan,
"5 Grosvenor Road, Rathmines."

"Ardgowan, Grosvenor Road,

"Rathmines, 6th September, 1882

"DEAR SIR—In reply to your inquiry, I beg to inform you that on the 16th August, shortly after I received the order of the court to take you into custody, Mr. Superintendent Ward came to me and said he was instructed to inform me that a police van was at my service to convey you to prison, I felt naturally indignant on my own account as well as upon yours, seeing which; Mr. Ward said 'Sir, I am merely discharging my duty in conveying to you the message.' I then procured at my own expense the best vehicle I could get at a short notice.

"I am, dear Sir,

"Yours very faithfully,

"NICHOLAS C. WHTTE,

"Coroner, Dublin City.

"E. D. GRAY, ESQ., M.P.,

"High Sheriff of Dublin,

"Richmond Prison."

THE SEPARATION OF THE JURY.

——:o:——

The following extracts referring to the separation of the jury, are quoted from the sworn affidavit of A. Martin, furnished to his Excellency. The other portions of the affidavit referring to the jury, as well as the affidavits sworn by other persons on the same subject, are not given here, because the jury swore counter affidavits which are not accessible to the Committee, and the Committee do not desire to publish one set of affidavits without the others. But they have no difficulty in publishing that portion of the affidavit of A. Martin dealing with the question of the separation of the jury and their mixing with the public, because the assertion that they did so separate, and did so mix, has never been questioned in public, and, in fact, is acknowledged in the letter from Mr. Hamilton, one of the jury quoted below :—

"I, Alfred Martin, twenty-one years of age and upwards, Billiard-marker at the Imperial Hotel, Sackville-street, Dublin, make oath and say, that on Friday night, the 11th inst., I saw six men, whom I knew to be members of the jury in the case of the Queen v. Hynes, in the public billiard-room. I do not know where the rest of the jury were at the time, but they were not in the billiard-room. There were four persons in the billiard-room at the time who were not members of the jury. They were Mr. Bushe, Major Wynne, Dr. Cusack, and another stranger—a friend of Mr. Reis's. I saw the jurors mixing with other persons who were not members of the jury. Mr. Reis handicapped a game of billiards in which persons not jurors were playing.

* * * * * * *

"ALFRED R. MARTIN."

"Sworn before me this 17th day of August, 1882, at the Imperial Hotel, Lower Sackville-street, in the County of the City of Dublin, a Commissioner for taking Affidavits in the Supreme Court of Judicature in Ireland, and I know the deponent.

"JOHN STONE, Commissioner."

E

"THE JURORS IN THE HYNES CASE.

"TO THE EDITOR OF THE 'DAILY EXPRESS.'

"SIR—Being one of the jurors in the case of the Crown *versus* Hynes, I think it right to lay before you what actually did occur at the Imperial Hotel on Friday evening, the 11th inst.

"On the court rising at half-past five o'clock, the presiding judge directed the Sub-Sheriff to take charge of us for the night, and suggested that we should be taken to the Gresham Hotel. We were all much surprised when the Sub-Sheriff told us to choose between the European and Imperial Hotels. Knowing that these were chiefly patronized by the Land League and Nationalist party, we all remonstrated, requesting to be taken to the Gresham or Shelbourne Hotel, some jurors stating they would prefer to pass the night in the room at the courthouse. The Sub-Sheriff, however, ended the matter by informing us we had no choice, and that, as we refused to go to the European, he would have us at once removed to the Imperial.

"On arriving at the hotel we were taken upstairs to a passage at the top of the house, which, we were informed by the Sub-Sheriff, had been reserved entirely for our separate use. We were then immediately taken down to a room, where dinner had been prepared for us. After dinner some of the jurors asked permission to smoke. I and some others asked if it were allowable that the smokers might go together to another room, as the evening was very close. No objection was raised to this, and the smokers were taken, under charge of the Sub-Sheriff, bailiffs, and police, to the billiard-room of the hotel. There they remained, with the Sub-Sheriff or his son, till they all went to bed together, shortly before 12 o'clock. This, I have since been informed, was irregular; but we were none of us aware that it was so at the time. I can only say that, as the Sub-Sheriff took us against our will to the Imperial Hotel, he could as easily, with the strong guard of bailiffs and police at his disposal, have prevented our separating as we did. On inquiry from the proprietor of the Imperial Hotel, I find that the whole charge against the jury is that one of their number, Mr. Reis, was under the influence of liquor when in the billiard-room, and afterwards behaved rather noisily when going to bed.

"The foreman of the jury (Mr. Barrett, of Kingstown) stated in open court on Monday morning, the 13th inst., that he saw the last of the jurors to bed, which he considered it his duty to do, and that none of them were in any way under the influence of drink.

"This statement can be confirmed by those who were present at the time—one of them, Mr. Phillips, of Grafton-street, being a total abstainer from intoxicating drinks. Major Wynne, one of those gentlemen not on the jury who were admitted into the billiard-room during the evening, also informs me that while there he saw none of the jurors under the influence of drink. The Sub-Sheriff and his son were there. If strangers were admitted into the billiard-room, it was their business to have had the jurors removed, who were under their charge, or to have arranged with the proprietor of the hotel that they should have had the room to themselves. As I have said before, I, and I believe all the other members of the jury, were perfectly unaware of what the rules were to be observed under the circumstances. Now, as to Mr. W. O'Brien's extraordinary story, I was awake in room No. 27, nearly opposite his, when the party from the billiard-room came upstairs. I heard Mr. Reis speaking and calling out loudly (I have since been informed for slippers), as is his custom. I heard him knock over a bath and put it up again with more noise than was absolutely necessary. Mr. Reis is short-sighted, and I am informed that at the time there was very little light in the passage. I heard some one go to two or three rooms knocking at and opening the doors ; but I heard no singing, nor did I hear anything to lead me to imagine that drunken people were stumbling about in the passage. As to the opening of the doors, the Sub-Sheriff had informed us that the passage was reserved entirely to ourselves We had not all selected our rooms before dinner, and I was not astonished that those last upstairs had some difficulty in finding a spare bed, particularly as it appears that, while some of the jury were doubled up two in a room, one had been reserved for the use of the editor or ex-editor of *United Ireland*. The Attorney-General has promised that a full inquiry is to be made into the circumstances of the case. This the jurors, one and all, are anxious should be made at once. I am certain that whatever may appear to be against us as a body in the affidavits of the billiard-marker, assistant porter, and waiter of the Imperial Hotel, and of Mr. Wm. O'Brien, will assume a very different appearance when these gentlemen are themselves subjected to cross-examination and confronted with facts.

" Yours faithfully,
"EDWARD C. HAMILTON,
" Half-pay Bengal Staff Corps.
" Everdingen, Orwell-road, August 20, 1882."
—*Daily Express, August 21st*, 1882.

Of course the facts here disclosed would never have come to light but for the publication in the *Freeman*.

THE HOTEL BILL.

——:o:——

"Richmond Jail,
"29th August, 1882.

" DEAR SIR—As some questions of importance have arisen in connection with the quantity of liquor supplied to the jury on the night of the 13th, in the case of the Queen v. Hynes, I have to request that you, as Sub-Sheriff, having charge of the jury, will furnish to me at once a vouched copy of the hotel bill for the jury on the night in question, specifying the prices, so that the quantity may be ascertained ; also, that you will state the number of bailiffs or other attendants upon the jury, and the quantity of drink supplied to them, which may be included in the bill, together with the names and addresses of those bailiffs or attendants. Please let me have this information early to-morrow, and oblige,

" Yours truly,

" E. DWYER GRAY, High Sheriff, .
" Dublin City.

" JAMES CAMPBELL, ESQ., Sub-Sheriff,
"20 Rutland Square, N."

————

" 8 Inns' Quay,
"1st September, 1882.

" DEAR SIR—In compliance with your request, I send you a copy of the hotel bill showing the quantity of drink supplied in the Hynes case, and also the quantity consumed by the constables and bailiffs in charge, as taken from their several declarations made yesterday and this morning.

" I am, truly yours,

" JAMES CAMPBELL.

" E. D. GRAY, ESQ., M.P."

JURY ACCOUNT. IMPERIAL HOTEL,
LOWER SACKVILLE STREET
(Opposite the General Post Office and Central Telegraph Station).
August 11th and 12th, 1882.

			£ s. d.	£ s. d.	
Brought forward.				10 0 1	
Apartments	...	For 12	36/-		
Attendance	...			18/-	
Breakfast	...	,,		{ 30/- { 12/-	For 12 For 6
Dinners	...	,,	48/-		Police and Bailiffs.
7 Ale and 1 Stout	...	8 pints	4/-		
Sherry	...	1 bottle	6/-		
Champagne	...	1 bottle	10/-		
Claret	...	3 bottles	12/-		
Burgundy	...				
Moselle or Hock	...				
Hollands	...	6 glasses	3/-		
Brandy	..	Half-glass	6d.		
Whiskey or Punch	...	32½ glasses	16/3	1/6	3 glasses
Cigars	...		8/2		
Tea or Coffee	...	For 12, & 2 cups }	18/- } 1/- } 19/-	1/-	{ 1 cup {and B. B
Gas	...		1/6		
Baths	...			4/-	
Messages	...			1/6	
Rum	...	2 glasses	1/-		
Sandwiches	...				
Aerated Waters	...	12 bottles	6/-	1/-	2 bottles
Stationery	...		2d.		
Sitting Room	...		7/6		
Police and Bailiffs—					
Dinners	...	For 6	15/-		
Suppers	...	For 6	6/-		
Carried forward.			£10 0 1	£13 9 1	

From this accompanying statement it appears that there were six attendants upon the jury—four policemen and two bailiffs. They all swore affidavits as to the quantity they consumed. The total between them amounted to five pints of beer, one pint of stout, and ten and a half glasses of spirits.

The following, taken from the Dublin *Daily Express*, gives the account of Mr. Hamilton, one of the jury, of the amount consumed by them :—

"THE JURY IN THE HYNES CASE.

"Mr. Edward Hamilton, one of the jurors, whose letter we published on this day week, says—I now enclose you a return showing the exact amount of spirits, &c., drunk by each of the jurors in the case of the Crown v. Hynes, taken from the jurors' affidavits. The beer, gin, and whiskey were drunk chiefly by the bailiffs and police, who had, of course, to be provided with refreshments at the hotel. An affidavit from each member of the jury has been submitted to his Excellency the Lord Lieutenant, which will effectually put an end to the slanderous calumnies which have been promulgated by the enemies of justice against us. In addition, there was one bottle of champagne between four—Mr. Barrett, Mr. M'Conkey, Mr. Reis, and Mr. Wardrope :—

	Beer.	Claret. (St. Estephe)	Sherry.	Spirits.
Charles Reis	—	3	—	1
William Barrett	—	—	5	—
G. Searight	—	3	0½	—
* E. Philips	—	—	—	—
* R. Carby	—	—	—	—
E. Hamilton	—	—	—	1
J. Beatey	—	1½	—	—
J. M'Conkey	—	4	—	—
William Gibson	3	—	0½	0½
W. Wardrope	—	—	1	2
W. Macklin	—	—	—	—
Richard Barbour	—	2	—	1
Total of glasses	3	18½	7	5½

"The names marked with asterisks are those of the jury who are total abstainers."

CONDUCT OF MR. MORPHY.

The following indicates that, although only a few hours' notice was given to Mr. Gray, his fate was anticipated, though Mr. Morphy did not give the true explanation to the gentleman who was summoned beforehand to take him into custody :—

" Richmond Jail,
" *Dublin, 4th, September,* 1882.

" DEAR SIR—I have been informed that Mr. Morphy, Crown Prosecutor for the Co. Clare, wrote to you on the evening of the 15th August requiring you to attend the Commission Court in Green Street on the morning of the 16th. I will be extremely obliged if you will let me have a copy of his letter. If I am correctly informed, although you were summoned to attend, in reality for the purpose of taking me into custody, this was not the pretext put forward in Mr. Morphy's letter.

"This is the point I wish to clear up.

" Yours truly,
" (Signed), E. DWYER GRAY.

" Dr. N. C. Whyte, City Coroner, 5 Grosvenor Road."

"Ardgowan, Grosvenor Road, Rathmines,
" *6th September,* 1882.

" DEAR SIR—In compliance with your request I enclose a copy of the letter received by me from the Crown Solicitor, Mr. Morphy, on the morning of the 16th August, 1882.

" Believe me, yours faithfully,
" NICHOLAS C. WHYTE, Coroner.

" EDMUND DWYER GRAY, ESQ., M.P.,
" High Sheriff, Dublin City."

[PRESSING.]

" 13 Lower Ormond Quay,
" *15th August,* 1882.

" DEAR SIR —I have been directed to request you to attend at the Commission Court, Green Street, at eleven o'clock to-morrow (Wednesday) morning, as the Solicitor General may have to refer to you for some official information.

" Faithfully yours,
" ALEXANDER MORPHY, Crown Solicitor.

" NICHOLAS WHYTE, ESQ.,
" Coroner Dublin City."

[" The above is a true copy. Nicholas C. Whyte, Coroner, *6th Sept.*"]

The following is the correspondence referred to (p. 12) as proving that Mr. Morphy had inquired into the accusations at the very time the Solicitor-General, who was instructed, and the Judge declared that they could not be inquired into :—

"THE JURY IN THE HYNES CASE.

" *October 4th,* 1882.

"DEAR SIR—Will you kindly say if it is a fact that Mr. Alexander Morphy, Crown Solicitor, called upon you on Monday, August the 14th, to make inquiries as to the statements contained in a letter published in the *Freeman's Journal* of that date by Mr. William O'Brien concerning the jury in the Hynes case.

" Yours faithfully, ·

" E. DWYER GRAY.

" CHARLES LAWLER, Esq.,
"Imperial Hotel."

" Imperial Hotel, Lower Sackville Street,
" *October* 4th, 1882.

" DEAR SIR—It is a fact that Mr. Alexander Morphy called on me on the 12th August with reference to the letter of Mr. O'Brien which appeared in the *Freeman's·Journal* of that date.

" I remain, yours truly,

CHARLES LAWLER.

" E. DWYER GRAY, Esq , M.P., High Sheriff."

— :0:——

THE JURIES AT THE SPECIAL COMMISSION,

3rd August, 1882.

——:o:——

CONSTITUTION OF THE JURIES.

The following gives the manner of constituting the jury panels :—

"Richmond Jail,
"Dublin, 18th September, 1882.

"DEAR SIR—"I will be obliged by your letting me know officially the precise manner in which the jury panel in the case of the present commission was made out by you on my behalf.

"Yours faithfully,
"E. DWYER GRAY.

"JAMES CAMPBELL, Esq., Sub-Sheriff,
"8, Inns' Quay."

———

"8 Inns' Quay,
"Dublin, 20th September, 1882.

"DEAR SIR—In reply to your letter of the 18th inst., requesting me to let you know the precise manner in which the special jury panel has been made out for the present Commission, I beg to inform you it has been done in strict conformity with the Prevention of Crimes Act, 1882, and the order in council made under the provisions of said act, and also under the provisions of the Juries' (Ireland) Acts of 1871, 1872, and 1876.

"These latter acts direct sheriffs to summon juries in a regular alphabetical eries by returning one name from each letter in succession, beginning with the first letter and so proceeding regularly through the letters of the alphabet rom first to last as often as may be necessary, and so far as the number of names in each letter will admit, until a sufficient number of names shall have been placed on the panel, taking care always to commence each new panel at the letter next following the last letter of the preceding panel.

"The panel you inquire about, like all others, since I came into office, was, I trust, in strict conformity with the above statutory requirements.

"I am,
"Very truly yours,
"JAMES CAMPBELL.

"E. DWYER GRAY, Esq., M.P."

Two panels were returned to try the cases : one for the county, the other for the city of Dublin, each containing 100 names.

COUNTY PANEL.

The county panel contains 63 Protestants and 37 Catholics.

Two of the jurors on this panel were dead at the time it was issued. Their names are Patrick B. Darcy, Dunedan, Monkstown, merchant (Catholic), and Edward Nolan, of Killeen Mills, Inchicore, paper merchant (Catholic).

Two jurors—Charles L. Reis, 1, Aylesbury-road, jeweller ; and J. B. Johnston, of Clyde-road, broker,—are also returned on the city panel. The first is a Jew, the second a Protestant.

Two jurors being dead, and two being also on the city panel, reduces the county panel to 96 available names, of which 61 are Protestants, and 35 Catholics.

THE PROTESTANTS ARE—

1. William Macklin, Crofton-terrace, Kingstown, plumber.
2. George A. Newcomen, 20 Leeson-park, gentleman.
3. William Parry, Salthill, Monkstown, hotel-keeper.
4. John Quain, 49 Pembroke-road, Dublin, stock-broker.
5. John H. Reid, Holmston-house, Kingstown, gentleman.
6. Captain Joseph Scovell, 1 St. John's-terrace, North Circular-road, retired captain.
7. David Waldie, Collinstown, Santry, farmer.
8. Robert F. Young, St. Margaret's, Dalkey, stock-broker.
9. Henry Alley, Maryvilla, Clonturk, Drumcondra, gentleman.
10. Richard D. Barber, 10 Grosvenor-road, West, bank manager
11. William Galbraith, Rathgar-road, Dublin, gentleman.
12. William James Halliday, Brookville, Monkstown, grocer.
13. John William Jameson, Lota, Blackrock, gentleman.
14. George Macnie, Baymount, Clontarf, printer and stationer.
15. George Newsome, Clapham-villas, merchant.
16. Dr. George V. Patton, 28 Burlington-road, LL.D., barrister.
17. Francis Moore Scott, Island-bridge, wool manufacturer, J.P.
18. Henry J. Vickers, Hermitage, Blackrock, barrister.
19. Robert R. Young, 8 Raglan-road, stock-broker.
20. Hugh Barr, Dodsborough, Lucan, farmer.
21. Captain George Carey, Laurel-lodge, Terenure, retired army officer.
22. Henry W. Figgis, 20 Grosvenor-road, merchant.
23. Robert Gardiner, Ashley-house, 6 Clyde-road, accountant.
24. Charles R. Hamilton, Belgrave-square, Monkstown, gentleman.
25. Francis Johnston, De Vesci-terrace, Monkstown, gentleman.
26. John Lebrary, Braganza, Dalkey, merchant.
27. John Maconchey, Highfield-road, gentleman.

28. Henry Nicholl, Bohamer, St. Dolough's, gentleman.
29. Benjamin J. Patterson, 64 Leeson-street, upper, architect.
30. Strattell Scott, 39 Mespil-road, veterinary surgeon.
31. Dean Conroy Taylor, Priory, Rathfarnham, gentleman.
32. Arthur W. Vincent, 9 Clyde-road, gentleman.
33. Hugh Wallace, Dunleary-road, Kingstown, merchant.
34. Beresford Anderson, Greenhill, Killiney, esquire.
35. John Barr, Belgard, farmer.
36. Richard Carey, 57 Lansdowne-road, gentleman.
37. Henry J. Finlay, Corkagh demesne, gentleman, J.P.
38. John Gailey, Palmerston-house, Rathmines, merchant.
39. Edward Hamilton, Orwell-road, gentleman.
40. Francis Johnston, Sloperton, Kingstown, gentleman.
41. Frederick W. Nevin, Silchester-road, Dundrum, bank official.
42. John Payne, 32 Palmerston-road, Cullenswood, merchant.
43. Graves E. Searight, 78 Pembroke-road, stock-broker.
44. William Wallace, Dunleary-road, Kingstown, coal merchant.
45. William George Barrett, Newtownsmith, Kingstown, merchant.
46. Henry Carleton, Seapoint-road, Monkstown, merchant.
47. Francis R. Davis, Hawthorne-lodge, Stillorgan, esquire.
48. Pierce Finucane, 19 Pembroke-road, gentleman.
49. Gowan R. Hamilton, Shanganagh Castle, Loughlinstown, militia officer.
50. John B. Johnston, 8 Clyde-road, baker.
51. John Lee, Vesci-place, Kingstown, farmer.
52. Goodricke L. Peacock, Coolamore-road, Dalkey, gentleman.
53. Charles L. Reis, 1 Aylesbury-road, jeweller.
54. Charles Thompson, 35 Leeson park, gentleman.
55. Charles Archer, Claremount-villas, Kingstown, gentleman.
56. Sir John Barrington, St. Anne's, Killiney, merchant.
57. J. Crichton Carleton, 62 Northumberland-road, stockbroker.
58. David Davis, 2 Rathmines, merchant.
59. Francis Fitzgerald, Churchtown, Dundrum, army officer.
60. Francis F. Gaynor, Killiney-house, Killiney, retired army officer.
61. Henry Alexander Hamilton, George's-street, Balbriggan, esquire, J.P.
62. Samuel Jolly, Merville, Stillorgan, farmer.
63. Edward Keegan, Verney, Golden Ball, farmer.

THE CATHOLICS ARE—

1. John O'Brien, Northumberland-avenue, Kingstown, gentleman.

2. Edward Taaffe, Upper George's-street, Kingstown, publican.
3. Hugh Vaughan, 9 Aylesbury-road, Sinnot's-court, merchant.
4. George Campbell, Hermitage, Harold's-grange, merchant.
5. Peter Daly, Maynetown, Baldoyle, farmer.
6. Denis Egan, Santry, farmer.
7. Thomas Fagan, Martello-terrace, Kingstown, gentleman.
8. John Kane, 10 and 11 Leeson-park, merchant.
9. John Lawler, Irishtown, Palmerston, farmer.
10. Joseph O'Brien, 2 Palmerston park, merchant.
11. Edward Reilly, Ballyman, Glasnevin, farmer.
12. Patrick Tallon, Collinstown, leather merchant.
13. Valentine Wall, Nutstown-house, landholder.
14. David Allingham, Seafield, Clontarf, merchant.
15. Louis Daniel, 10 Rathmines, merchant.
16. Edward Egan, Marine-terrace, Kingstown, merchant.
17. William D. Kane, DeVesci-terrace, Kingstown, gentleman.
18. Frederick O'Callaghan, Clonsilla, grazier.
19. James Reilly, Baldoyle, farmer.
20. Patrick B. Darcy, Dunedan, Monkstown, merchant (dead).
21. Laurence Egan, Riversdale-house, Monkstown, merchant.
22. James Kavanagh, Huntstown-house, Finglas, farmer.
23. William Ledwich, Ashfield, Clondalkin, farmer.
24. James Magee, 1 Terenure-road, Rathgar, grocer.
25. John Taylor, Lusk, farmer.
26. Joseph Archbold, Malahide, farmer.
27. James Ennis, Naul, farmer.
28. John Gavan, 71 Queen-street, auctioneer and factor.
29. Joseph Kearns, Cottage, Finglas, farmer.
30. Edward Maher, Balscadden, Balbriggan, farmer.
31. Edward Nolan, Killeen Mills, Inchicore, paper manufacturer (dead).
32. Roderick S. O'Connor, 88 Pembroke-road, gentleman.
33. Daniel Sexton, Eastmoreland-place, contractor.
34. Michael Walsh, Rookwood, Rathfarnham, stationer.
35. William Ennis, Clonare, Balbriggan, farmer.
36. Daniel O'Connor, Ward-house, Ward, grazier.
37. Patrick Reilly, Blundelstown, Clondalkin, grazier.

CITY PANEL.

The city panel contains the names of 51 Protestants, 48 Catholics, and one Jew—Mr. Charles L. Reis.

Of the Catholics two were dead—John McDermott, Mountjoy-square, West, druggist ; and Matthew Reynolds, Redmond's-hill, broker. One—Patrick Carroll, Stephen's-green, North,. iron-monger, also a Catholic—had left before the panel was issued.

The result is that the available city panel consisted of 97 names, of which 51 were Protestants, 45 Catholics, and one Jew.

THE PROTESTANTS ARE—

1. William M. Evans, 66 Grafton-street, stationer.
2. Alexander Ferrier, 59 William-street, merchant.
3. William Gibson, 14 Lower Ormond-quay, seedsman.
4. James Harrison, 17 Henry-street, confectioner.
5. Charles Johnston, 27 Upper Sackville-street, druggist.
6. Charles Leechman, 59 William-street, merchant.
7. George Nutter, 115 Grafton-street, print-seller.
8. Adam Phayre, 6 Hume-street, lodginghouse-keeper.
9. Robert Sexton, 51 Dawson-street, tailor.
10. George B. Thompson, 9 and 10 Eustace-street, wine merchant.
11. Thomas H. Ward, Riverview, Conyngham-road, gentleman.
12. George Atkinson, 5 William-street, merchant.
13. George H. Beare, 11 Conyngham-road, gentleman.
14. George Carolan, 82½ Talbot-street, builder.
15. Thomas Fetherston, 143 Great Britain-street, chandler.
16. Thomas Gilbert, 18 Westmoreland-street, merchant tailor.
17. Edmund Johnston, 94 Grafton-street, goldsmith.
18. Thomas Leetch, 56 Dame-street, magistrate.
19. Thomas Nuzum, 201 Great Brunswick-street, coal merchant.
20. Alexander Ogilvy, 13 Grafton-street, draper.
21. William J. H. Reside, 20 College-green, cloth merchant.
22. Walter Sexton, 118 Grafton-street, jeweller.
23. John D. Wardell, 75 Thomas-street, tea merchant.
24. George P. Beater, 17 Lower Sackville-street, druggist.
25. Denis J. Field, 9 Westmoreland-street, stationer.
26. Edward Johnston, 43 Grafton-street, restaurant keeper.
27. Wills Phenix, 10 Leinster-street, gas-fitter.
28. Abraham Shackleton, 35A James's-street, West, corn-merchant.
29. Archibald Wardlaw, 10 D'Olier-street, gentleman.
30. Orlando Beater, 11 to 15 Henry-street, gentleman.
31. Henry Fielding, 33 Dawson-street, tabinet manufacturer.
32. James Sproule Johnson, 16 Lower Ormond-quay, wholesale paper merchant.
33. Adam F. Macdonald, 65 South Gt. George's-street, draper.
34. Ephraim Phillips, 37 Grafton-street, draper.
35. James Shanks, 54 Townsend-street, mineral water manufacturer.
36. Thomas Wardrop, jun., 55 Gt. Brunswick-street, builder.
37. James Beatty, 20 Grafton-street, merchant.
38. Samuel Figgis, 104 Grafton-street, bookseller.
39. John B. Johnston, 5 Townsend-street, merchant.
40. Graham Lemon, 49 Lower Sackville-street, confectioner.

41. Thomas Phillips, 18 North Earl-street, bootmaker.
42. Haughton W. Shannon, 108 and 109 Thomas-street, haberdasher.
43. William Thompson, 17 Talbot-street, reporter.
44. William Wardrop, 55 Great Brunswick-street, builder.
45. John Beatty, 14 Grafton-street, carpet manufacturer.
46. Arthur Denny, 66 Lower Leeson-street, gentleman.
47. Adam S. Findlater, 29 Upper Sackville-street, wine merchant.
48. Wilfred Haughton, 27 and 28 City-quay, corn merchant.
49. Joseph G. Lendrum, 29 Thomas-street, tobacco manufacturer.
50. Thomas Phillips, 4 Dame-street, tailor.
51. Robert W. Richan, 145 Great Britain-street, grocer.

THE CATHOLICS ARE—

1. Philip Carlin, 91 Lower Baggot-street, gentleman.
2. William H. Delany, 85 and 86 Coombe, pawnbroker.
3. John C. Kelly, 14 Cope-street, wholesale merchant.
4. Alphonsus M'Dermott, 65 Great Britain-street, wine merchant.
5. Patrick O'Farrell, 145 North King-street, tobacconist.
6. Peter Dempsey, 5 Nassau-street, draper.
7. James Hart, 2 Henry-street, bootmaker.
8. John J. Kelly, 39 Sackville-street, grocer.
9. John M'Dermott, 64 Mountjoy-square, West, druggist.
10. Henry Phelan, 43 Denzille-street, house painter.
11. John Thompson, 45 Dawson-street, saddler.
12. Peter Aungier, 22 Dominick-street, salesmaster.
13. James Carolan, 26 to 30 Amiens-street, hotel-keeper.
14. Cornelius Dennehy, 41 Mountjoy-square, South, gentleman, J.P.
15. Andrew Gilligan, 9 College-street, vintner.
16. Joseph C. Hart, 19 and 20 Pill-lane, vintner.
17. Joseph Kelly, 66 and 67 Thomas-street, timber merchant.
18. John Lemass, 2 Capel-street, hatter.
19. William M'Dermott, 65 Great Britain-street, wine merchant.
20. Jeremiah O'Hare, 35 Dolphin's-barn-lane, tanner.
21. Bernard Reynolds, 61 Capel-street, grocer.
22. Patrick Thompson, 85 Lower Gardiner-street, wine merchant.
23. Robert Aungier, 22 Lower Dominick-street, salesmaster.
24. James Carr, 14 Copper-alley, provision merchant.

25. Thomas Dennehy, 56 and 57 Lower Baggot-street, coach-builder.
26. Philip Gilligan, 78 Middle Abbey-street, vintner.
27. John Haughey, 8 Lower Bridge-street, hardware merchant.
28. Martin Kelly, 39 Upper Sackville-street, grocer.
29. Edward Lenehan, 27 Castle-street, leather merchant.
30. Edward O'Leary, 42 Stephen-street, grocer.
31. Mathew Reynolds, 1 and 2 Redmond's-hill, broker.
32. William Thompson, 85 Lower Gardiner-st., wine merchant
33. Robert Aungier, 70 Eccles-street, esquire.
34. Patrick Carroll, 18 Stephen's-green, North, ironmonger.
35. William Dennehy, 9 and 10 John-street, West, wholesale wine and spirit merchant.
36. Patrick M. Gleeson, 28 Thomas-street, grocer.
37. Patrick Haughey, 4 Lower Bridge-street, hardware merchant.
38. Peter Kelly, 1 and 2 Wood-quay, wine and spirit merchant.
39. James M'Donald, 62 Upper Dorset-street, provision dealer.
40. Michael O'Loughlin, 20 South Richmond-street, butcher.
41. Patrick Reynolds, 51 South Great George's-street, grocer.
42. Thomas Aungier, 70 Eccles-street, esquire.
43. William B. Carroll, 14 Mary-street, grocer.
44. Jeremiah Goggin, 74 Grafton-street, bog-oak manufacturer.
45. Robert M. Johnston, 68 Lower Mount-street, wine merchant.
46. William Kelly, 56 Sackville-street, fishing tackle manufacturer.
47. John M'Donald, 10 Lower Gardiner-street, tailor.
48. Michael O'Meara, 51 Thomas-street, grocer.

The two panels, county and city, contained 193 names, of which 112 were Protestants, 80 Catholics, and one a Jew.

MODE OF SELECTING A JURY.

The mode in which a particular jury is selected is as follows : The whole panel is called upon. There is a number opposite the name of each juror on the panel. The numbers corresponding to the names of those who answer are put into a ballot box. They are drawn one by one, and if not challenged or told `to stand aside are sworn, this process going on until twelve are sworn.

THE O'CONNOR JURY.

The first article in the *Freeman's Journal* relating to the composition of the juries at the special commission appeared on Friday the 11th August. It was a brief paragraph, referring to the case of the Queen *v.* John O'Connor and others—" The Kerry Outrage Case"—which had been at hearing the previous day, and stating the Crown exercised their right to challenge " on a wholesale scale," and no less than nineteen persons, some of them among our most respectable citizens, were ordered to " stand aside." ·

The jurors ordered to stand aside were :—

1. Hugh Vaughan, Aylesbury-road, merchant ... Catholic.
2. James Ennis, Naul, farmer ... Catholic.
3. Thomas Phillips, Dame-street, tailor ... Protestant.
4. W. H. Delany, the Coombe, pawnbroker .. Catholic.
5. John Lemass, Capel-street, hatter ... Catholic.
6. Joseph Archbold, Malahide, farmer ... Catholic.
7. Edward Lenehan, Castle-st., leather merchant Catholic.
8. William Ledwich, Clondalkin, farmer ... Catholic.
9. James Magee, Terenure-road, grocer ... Catholic.
10. Martin Kelly, Upper Sackville-street, grocer Catholic.
11. Patrick Reilly, Clondalkin, grazier ... Catholic.
12. Edward O'Leary, Stephen-street, grocer ... Catholic.
13. William Dennehy, John-st., West, merchant Catholic.
14. John Taylor, Lusk, farmer ... ... Catholic.
15. William Thompson, Talbot street, reporter ... Protestant.
16. Jeremiah O'Hare, Dolphin's-barn-lane, tanner Catholic.
17. Patrick Reynolds, Sth. Gt. George-st., grocer Catholic.
18. Philip Carlin, Lower Baggot-street, gentleman Catholic.
19. Louis Daniel, Rathmines, grocer ... ... Catholic.
20. James Carolin, Amiens-street, hotel-keeper... Catholic.

Note.—The *Freeman* article said nineteen were set aside. The printed report shows twenty, as above.

Of the twenty thus set aside, eighteen were Catholics and two Protestants.

The prisoners challenged the following six jurors—all Protestants :—

1. John Maconchey, Highfield-road, gentleman Protestant.
2. William Gibson, 14 Lower Ormond-quay, seedsman ... ... Protestant.
3. John Beatty, 14 Grafton-street, carpet manufacturer ... ... Protestant.
4. Samuel Figgis, 104 Grafton-street, bookseller Protestant.
5. Ephraim Phillips, 37 Grafton-street, draper Protestant.
6. Graves E. Searight, 78 Pembroke-road, stock-broker ... ... Protestant.

The jury who tried the case were :—

1. John Lebrary, Braganza, Dalkey, merchant Protestant,
2. William George Barrett, Newtownsmith, Kingstown, wine merchant... ... Protestant.

3. Francis Johnston, Sloperton, Kingstown,
gentleman ... ... Protestant.
4. James Shanks, Townsend-street, mineral
water manufacturer ... ... Protestant.
5. John Payne, 32 Palmerston-road, Cullenswood, merchant ... ... Protestant.
6. Thomas Wardrop, 55 Great Brunswick-
street, builder ... ... Protestant.
_7. Adam S. Findlater, Sackville-street, upper,
wine merchant... ... ... Protestant.
8. William Wallace, Dunleary-road, Kingstown, coal merchant ... ... Protestant.
9. Wills Phenix, 10 Leinster-street, gas-fitter Protestant.
10. Haughton W. Sharman, 108 and 109 Thomas-
street, haberdasher ... ... Protestant.
11. Thomas Fetherstone, 143 Great Britain-
street, chandler ... ... Protestant.
12. George P. Beater, 17 Sackville-street, lower,
druggist ... ... Protestant.

The jury was exclusively composed of Protestants.

THE HYNES JURY.

The second article in the *Freeman's Journal* appeared on Saturday, August 12th, and referred to the fact that in the above case,
which was still at trial, the Crown had set aside, as in the previous
case, a large number of Catholic jurors.

In this case 49 names were drawn, consisting of 22
Catholics, 26 Protestants, and one Jew. The prisoner challenged
11 Protestants, leaving 15 Protestants, one Jew, and 22 Catholics.
The Crown "set aside" 4 Protestants and the entire 22 Catholics,
leaving a jury consisting of 11 Protestants, one Jew, and no
Catholics.

In this case the Crown set aside the following :—

1. William Dennehy, John-street, West,
merchant ... ... Catholic.
2. Edward O'Leary, Stephen-street, grocer ... Catholic.
3. Patrick Reilly, Clondalkin, grazier ... Catholic.
4. Martin Kelly, Upper Sackville-street, grocer Catholic.
5. James Magee, Terenure-road, grocer ... Catholic.
6. William Ledwich, Clondalkin, farmer ... Catholic.
7. Edward Lenehan, Castle-st., leather merchant Catholic.
8. Joseph Archbold, Malahide, farmer ... Catholic.

F

9. John Lemass, 2 Capel-street, hatter ... Catholic.
10. W. H. Delany, the Coombe, pawnbroker ... Catholic.
11. Michael O'Loughlin, South Richmond-street,
    butcher ... ... Catholic.
12. Thomas Leetch, Dame-street, china merchant Protestant.
13. John J. Kelly, Upper Sackville-street, grocer Catholic.
14. Patrick Haughey, 4 Bridge-street, lower,
    hardware merchant ... ... Catholic.
15. James Reilly, Baldoyle, farmer ... ... Catholic.
16. Thomas Phillips, Dame-street, tailor Protestant.
17. Andrew Gilligan, College-street, vintner ... Catholic.
18. Peter Aungier, Dominick-street, salesmaster Catholic.
19. James Carolin, Amiens-street, hotel-keeper ... Catholic.
20. Adam Phayre, Hume-street, lodginghouse-
    keeper ... ... Protestant.
21. Peter Dempsey, Nassau-street, draper ... Catholic.
22. Laurence Egan, Riversdale, Monkstown,
    shopkeeper ... . Catholic.
23. Louis Daniel, Rathmines, grocer ... Catholic.
24. Patrick O'Farrell, North King-st., tobacconist Catholic.
25. Thomas Phillips, North Earl-st., bootmaker Protestant.
26. Philip Carlin, Baggot-street, gentleman .. Catholic.

Of the twenty-six jurors ordered to stand aside, twenty-two were Catholics and four Protestants.

The "challenges" by the prisoner were:—

1. Walter Sexton, Grafton-street, jeweller ... Protestant.
2. Capt. George Carey, Laurel-lodge, Terenure Protestant.
3. Alexander O'Gilvy, Grafton-street, draper Protestant.
4. James Beatty, Grafton-street, merchant ... Protestant.
5. Francis Johnston, De Vesci-terrace,
   Kingstown, gentleman ... ... Protestant.
6. Francis M. Scott, Kilmainham, woollen
   manufacturer ... ... Protestant.
7. Henry Finlay, Corcagh demesne, gentleman Protestant.
8. Samuel Figgis, Grafton-street bookseller ... Protestant.
9. Edmund Johnson, Grafton-road, goldsmith Protestant.
10. George Macnie, Baymount, Clontarf, printer Protestant.
11. George B. Thompson, Eustace-street, wine
    merchant ... ... Protestant.

All the above eleven jurors challenged by the prisoner were Protestants.

The jury actually sworn were as follows:—

1. Charles Reis, silversmith, Grafton-street ... Jew.
2. William G. Barrett, Kingstown, merchant ... Protestant.
3. Graves Searight, Pembroke-rd., stock-broker Protestant.

4. Ephraim Phillips, Grafton-street, draper ... Protestant.
5. Richard Carey, Lansdowne-road, gentleman Protestant.
6. Edward Hamilton, Orwell-road, gentleman Protestant.
7. John Beatty, Grafton-st., carpet manufacturer Protestant.
8. John Maconchey, Highfield park, gentleman... Protestant.
9. Wm. Wardrop, Great Brunswick-st., builder Protestant.
10. Wm. Macklin, Kingstown, plumber ... Protestant.
11. R. D. Barber,Grosvenor-rd., W., bank manager Protestant.
12. Wm. Gibson, Ormond-quay, lower, seedsman Protestant.

Juror No. 6—Edward Hamilton, of Orwell-road, is and was at the time of the trial Secretary or Agent of the County of Dublin Property Defence Association, a branch of the Central Defence Association for Ireland. He is also a retired army officer on half-pay. This is the juror who wrote the letters defending the jury in the newspapers.

PATRICK WALSH'S JURY—FIRST TRIAL.

On the 16th August Patrick Walsh was placed on his trial for the murder of Martin Lydon at Letterfrack. Owing to the mode adopted by the officials of the Crown, it was impossible to ascertain the names of the jurors who were ordered to "stand by," as the moment the Clerk of the Crown called out the number prefixed to the juror's name on the printed panels Mr. Anderson, a Crown official (who being seated alongside, knew what juror was about to be called) exclaimed "stand by" without waiting for the name, and conse-quently the Clerk of the Crown omitted to call the names of those jurors altogether. Had the names of all the jurors been comprised in one panel, the omission to call the name would not have mattered, as the number would have enabled the juror to be ascertained. But there being two panels —one for the county and one for the city—and each panel being numbered separately from 1 to 100, the result of directing a number to stand aside instead of a name was effectually to prevent the press and the public from knowing what jurors were ordered to stand aside. We can, therefore, only give the names of the jurors who were sworn.

THE JURY SWORN WAS COMPOSED OF THE FOLLOWING :—

1. James Beatty, 20 Grafton-street, merchant ... Protestant.
2. Francis Johnson, DeVesci-terrace, Monkstown
   accountant-general, Bank of Ireland ... Protestant.
3. William Gibson, 14 Lower Ormond-quay, seedsman ... ... Protestant.
4. James Harrison, 17 Henry-street, confectioner Protestant.

F2

5. Richard Carey, 57 Lansdowne-road, gentleman   Protestant.
6. William J. H. Reside, 20 College-green, cloth
    merchant   ...   . Protestant.
7. David Davis, Rathmines, merchant   ... Protestant.
8. Pierce Finucane, 19 Pembroke-road, gentleman Protestant.
9. W. James Halliday, Brookville, Monkstown,
    grocer   ...   . Protestant.
10. John B. Johnston, 8 Clyde-road, baker ... Protestant.
11. Wills Phenix, 10 Leinster-street, gas-fitter Protestant.
12 William Wallace, Dunleary-road, Kingstown,
    coal merchant ...   . Protestant.

The above Jury was exclusively Protestant. They were unable to agree to a verdict, and the prisoner was put back to be tried again.

PATRICK WALSH'S JURY—SECOND TRIAL.

Patrick Walsh was put upon his trial for the second time on the 21st August.

The Crown officials on this occasion reverted to the usual procedure, and called the name of each juror who was set aside.

The Crown ordered 20 jurors to stand aside, and 11 were challenged by the prisoner.

The following are the names of those who were ordered to stand by :—
1. John M'Donald, 10 Lower Gardiner-street,
    tailor   ...   . Catholic.
2. Samuel Jolly, Merville, Stillorgan, farmer ... Protestant.
3. Martin Kelly, 39 Upper Sackville-street,
    grocer   ...   . Catholic.
4. William B. Carroll, 14 Mary-street, grocer... Catholic.
5. James Ennis, Naul, farmer ...   ... Catholic.
6. Peter Dempsey, 5 Nassau-street, draper ... Catholic.
7. Thomas Aungier, 70 Eccles-street, esquire ... Catholic.
8. Arthur Denny, 66 Lower Leeson-street,
    gentleman   ...   . Protestant.
9. William Macklin, Crofton-terrace, Kingstown,
    plumber   ...   . Protestant.
10. Thomas Leetch, 56 Dame-street, magistrate... Protestant.
11. Hugh Wallace, Dunleary-road, Kingstown,
    merchant   ...   . Protestant.
12. Thomas Phillips, 4 Dame-street, tailor ... Protestant.
13. Edward Keegan, Verney, Golden Ball, farmer Protestant.
14. James C. Hart, 19 and 20 Pill-lane, vintner Catholic.
15. Andrew Gilligan, 9 College-street, vintner Catholic.
16. Graves E. Searight, 78 Pembroke-road,
    stock-broker   ...   . Protestant.

17. James M'Donald, 62 Upper Dorset-street,
    provision dealer ... ... Catholic.
18. Patrick M'Gleeson, 28 Thomas-street, grocer Catholic.
19. Robert W. Richan, 145 Great Britain-street,
    grocer ... ... Protestant.
20. Michael O'Loughlin, 20 South Richmond-st.,
    butcher ... ... Catholic.

Of the twenty jurors ordered to stand by, eleven were Catholics and nine Protestants.

The jurors challenged by the prisoner were :—

1. Francis M. Scott, Island-bridge, Kilmainham,
   J.P., wool manufacturer ... ... Protestant.
2. Joseph G. Lendrum, 29 Thomas-st., tobacco
   manufacturer ... ... Protestant.
3. John Beatty, 14 Grafton-street, carpet
   manufacturer ... ... Protestant.
4. Denis J. Field, 9 Westmoreland-street,
   stationer ... ... Protestant.
5. Henry Nicholl, Bohamer, St. Dolough's,
   gentleman ... ... Protestant.
6. Captain George Carey, Laurel-lodge, Terenure,
   retired army officer ... ... Protestant.
7. Charles Johnston, 27 Upper Sackville-street,
   druggist ... ... Protestant.
8. George Macnie, Baymount, Clontarf, printer
   and stationer ... ... Protestant.
9. Henry Alexander Hamilton, George's-street,
   Balbriggan, esquire, J.P. ... ... Protestant.
10. Ephraim Phillips, 37 Grafton-street, draper Protestant.
11. Robert Sexton, 51 Dawson-street, tailor ... Protestant.

The above eleven jurors are all Protestants.

The following comprised the jury who tried the case :—

1. William M. Evans, 66 Grafton-street,
   stationer ... ... Protestant.
2. George B. Thompson, 9 and 10 Eustace-street,
   wine merchant ... ... Protestant.
3. Richard D. Barber, 10 Grosvenor-road, West,
   bank manager ... ... Protestant.
4. Alexander Ogilvy, 13 Grafton-street, draper Protestant.
5. George Carolan, 82½ Talbot-street, builder Protestant.
6. Thomas Gilbert, 18 Westmoreland-street,
   merchant tailor ... ... Protestant.
7. Strattell Scott, 39 Mespil-road, veterinary
   surgeon ... ... Protestant.
8. Charles Leechman, 59 William-street,
   merchant ... ... Protestant.

9. John H. Reid, Holmston house, Kingstown,
   gentleman ... ... Protestant.
10. Edward Johnston, 48 Grafton-street,
    restaurant keeper ... ... Protestant.
11. George P. Beater, 17 Lower Sackville-street,
    Druggist ... ... Protestant.
12. John Maconchey, Highfield-road, gentleman Protestant.
The above jurors are all Protestants.

MICHAEL WALSH'S JURY.

The trial of Michael Walsh for the murder of Constable Kavanagh at Letterfrack, commenced on Wednesday, 27th September.

In this case the Crown set aside seventeen jurors, and eight were challenged by the prisoner.

THE JURORS ORDERED TO STAND BY WERE—

1. Edward O'Leary, 42 Stephen-street, grocer Catholic.
2. William Ledwich, Ashfield, Clondalkin,
   farmer ... ... Catholic.
3. Andrew Gilligan, 9 College-street, vintner Catholic.
4. James Carolan, 26 to 30 Amiens-street, hotel-
   keeper ... ... Catholic.
5. Henry J. Vickers, Hermitage, Blackrock,
   barrister ... ... Protestant.
6. Michael O'Loughlin, 20 South Richmond-
   street, butcher ... ... Catholic.
7. James Ennis, Naul, farmer ... ... Catholic.
8. Edward Reilly, Ballyman, Glasnevin, farmer Catholic.
9. William B. Carroll, 14 Mary-street, grocer Catholic.
10. Abraham Shackleton, 35A James's-street,
    West, corn merchant .. ... Protestant.
11. John Lawlor, Irishtown, Palmerston,
    farmer ... ... Catholic.
12. Martin Kelly, 39 Upper Sackville-street,
    grocer ... ... Catholic.
13. Joseph C. Hart, 19 and 20 Pill-lane,
    vintner ... ... Catholic.
14. Denis Egan, Santry, farmer ... ... Catholic.
15. Edward Taaffe, Upper George's-street,
    Kingstown, licensed publican ... ... Catholic.
16. Edward Egan, Marine-terrace, Kingstown Catholic.
17. Louis Daniel, 10 Rathmines, merchant ... Catholic.
Two of the above jurors are Protestants and 15 Catholics.

THE JURORS CHALLENGED BY THE PRISONER WERE—

1. Edward Hamilton, Orwell-road, gentleman — Protestant.
2. Henry J. Finlay, Corkagh demesne, gentleman, J.P. ... ... Protestant.
3. William Wallace, Dunleary-road, Kingstown, coal merchant ... ... Protestant.
4. W. J. H. Reside, 20 College-green, cloth merchant ... ... Protestant.
5. Edward Johnston, 43 Grafton-street, restaurant keeper ... ... Protestant.
6. Robert R. Young, 8 Raglan-road, stock-broker — Protestant.
7. Pierce Finucane, 19 Pembroke-road, gentleman — Protestant.
8. George Macnie, Baymount, Clontarf, printer and stationer ... ... Protestant.

The following twelve gentlemen composed the jury who tried Michael Walsh :—

1. Francis Johnston, Serpentine, Kingstown, gentleman ... ... Protestant.
2. Henry Fielding, 33 Dawson-street, tabinet manufacturer ... ... Protestant.
3. Denis J. Field, 9 Westmoreland-street, stationer ... ... Protestant.
4. William G. Barrett, Newtown Smith, Kingstown, wine merchant .. ... Protestant.
5. John B. Johnston, 8 Clyde-road, baker ... Protestant.
6. James Shanks, 54 Townsend-street, mineral water manufacturer ... ... Protestant.
7. Thomas Wardrop, junior, 55 Great Brunswick-street, builder ... ... Protestant.
8. Thomas Nuzum, 201 Great Brunswick-street, coal merchant ... ... Protestant.
9. William James Halliday, Brookville, Monkstown, grocer ... ... Protestant.
10. Wilfred Haughton, 27 and 28 City-quay, corn merchant ... ... Protestant.
11. Thomas Phillips, 4 Dame-street, tailor ... Protestant.
12. Henry W. Figgis, 20 Grosvenor-road, merchant ... ... Protestant.

The jury who tried the prisoner were all Protestants. Mr. Halliday (No 9 on the list), affirmed as a Quaker.

Subsequent to the comments in the *Freeman's Journal* calling attention to the exclusive non-Catholic composition of the juries a marked change is apparent in the course taken by the Crown. Proof of this is appended.

THE DECLARATION OF CATHOLIC JURORS.

The following is the full text of the declaration read, in the course of the debate, in the House of Commons, on August 17th, in reference to the sentence of Mr. Justice Lawson on Mr. E. D. Gray, M.P.:—

"We, the undersigned Catholic jurors of the city of Dublin, summoned to attend the Commission Court now sitting in Green-street, and ordered to stand aside by the Crown on Thursday and Friday last, hereby declare our belief that we were so ordered to stand aside solely on the ground that we were Catholics ; and we further declare we came to the conclusion at the time when so set aside, and prior to and quite independent of any comments in the *Freeman's Journal* on the subject" :—

Hugh Vaughan, 9 Aylesbury-road, Merrion.
Laurence Egan, 87 North King-street, and Riversdale, Queen's-park, Monkstown.
Patrick O'Farrell, 145 to 149 North King-street, and 24 Rutland-square.
Edward Lenehan, 27 and 28 Castle-street, and 1 Saint Edward's-terrace, Rathgar.
William Dennehy, 9 and 10 John-street, West, and 42 Mountjoy-square, South.
James Magee, 21 Lincoln-place, and 1 Terenure-road.
Louis Daniel, 10 Rathmines, and Valetta, Zion-road, Rathgar.
John J. Kelly, 89 Upper Sackville-street.
Martin Kelly, 89 Upper Sackville-street.
Patrick Haughey, 4, 5, and 6 Bridge-street, and 41 Cook-street.
John Lemass, 2 Capel-street

MEMORIAL TO LORD LIEUTENANT

IN

THE CASE OF FRANCIS HYNES.

——:o:——

The following is a copy of a memorial presented to His Excellency the Lord Lieutenant, on Saturday, 26th August, 1882, by the Solicitor of Francis Hynes:—

"TO HIS EXCELLENCY EARL SPENCER, K.G., LIEUTENANT GENERAL AND GENERAL GOVERNOR OF IRELAND.

"The humble memorial of John Frost, No. 6 Upper Ormond-quay, in the City of Dublin, Solicitor, respectively showeth unto your Excellency—

" 1. Your memorialist acted as Solicitor for Francis Hynes on his trial for the murder of one John Doloughty, which trial took place at Green-street Court-house, in this city, before the Right Honourable Mr. Justice Lawson and a jury, on 13th and 14th days of the present month of August. The said trial resulted in a verdict of guilty, whereupon the learned judge sentenced the said Francis Hynes to be executed on the 11th September, prox.

" 2. Your memorialist humbly submits to your Excellency that the said sentence should not be carried into effect for the following reasons and on the following grounds.

" 3. The trial commenced on the 13th instant, and on the evening of that day the court adjourned without finishing the cause. The Jury was given into the charge of special bailiffs to whom was administered an oath in the words following, that is to say :—' You shall not allow any person to have communication with the jury, save through the Sheriff, with the permission of the court, nor shall you allow the jury to separate or go at large until after the sitting of the court, pursuant to adjournment to be made for that purpose.'

" 4. The jury then retired to the Imperial Hotel in this city, accompanied by the special bailiffs. Your Excellency has been forwarded eleven affidavits sworn by eleven different persons, all residents or servants in the hotel, all having the amplest opportunity of observing the events of that night, and all having no interest whatever in the trial. Your memorialist submits to your

Excellency's consideration the statements as to the occurrences in the hotel in these affidavits contained.

" 5. Your memorialist further humbly submits to your Excellency that there is one most important point about which there is in effect no controversy whatever.

" 6. It appears from the testimony of several of the persons who made affidavits that no attempt even was made to keep the jurors together in the hotel, and separate from and without communication with the rest of the world. That the said jurors were permitted to go where they pleased in the hotel, and conversed with whomsoever they thought proper. That six of the jury entered the public billiard-room of the hotel, and remained there for over three hours, thus separating themselves from their fellows, who remained in another room of the hotel. That members of the outside public passed freely in and out of the billiard-room when the jurors were there. That one of the jurors was in close con versation with Major Wynne, a member of the outside public. That the said juror actually handicapped a game of billiards in which members of the outside public were playing. That the jurors in the billiard-room mixed freely with the outside public in the room.

" 7. Your memorialist humbly submits that these facts are substantially placed beyond all controversy by the letter voluntarily addressed to the 'public Press by Major Hamilton, one of the jurors, a copy of which is herewith sent to your Excellency. In that letter Major Hamilton does not deny any allegation as to the jurors mixing with the outside public in the billiard-room. He, in fact, admits the substantial accuracy of this part of the case.

" 8. In view of the foregoing facts your memorialist is advised that his client's remedy lies in this appeal to your Excellency, as the authority with whom rests the discretion of carrying out or not carrying out the sentence. Such was, your memorialist is advised, the decision in the case of the Queen v. Michael Murphy—Law Reports, 2nd Privy Council Appeals, page 35 and 535. In that case a prisoner, having been tried and convicted of a capital felony by a Court of Oyer and Terminer in New South Wales, and sentence of death passed, an application was made to the Supreme Court of New South Wales for a rule of *venire de novo* on an affidavit which stated that one of the jury had informed the deponent that, pending the trial and before verdict, the jury having adjourned to a hotel, had access to newspapers which contained a report of the trial as it proceeded, with comments thereon. The Supreme Court of New South Wales made a rule of *venire de novo*, Sir Alfred Stephen, the Chief Justice of New South Wales, in his judgment, declaring that the bailiffs sworn to take charge of the jury thereby became in fact officers of the Crown. The order of the New South Wales Court was subsequently reversed on technical grounds by the Judicial Committee of the Privy Council ; but in delivering the judgment of the Privy Council Sir William Erle said—'If irregularity occurs in the conduct of a trial not constituting a ground for treating the verdict as a nullity, the remedy to prevent a failure of justice is by application to the authority with whom rests the discretion either of executing the law or commuting the sentence. As there was, in the opinion of the Court below, irregularity in the trial of the respondent sufficient to vacate the judgment, their lordships have no doubt that, upon proper application on behalf of the respondent, which they recommend to be made, such weight will be given to these remarks as they may appear to deserve.' Your memorialist has not been able to obtain any official record of the fact, but he is informed, and verily believes, that in the above case of the Queen v. Murphy the sentence on the convict was at once commuted. There will doubtless be within your Excellency's reach ample means of informing yourself correctly on this point.

"9. It is humbly submitted to your Excellency that the separation of the jury in the present case and their free commerce and communication with the outside public was a miscarriage of justice and a violation of law. Your memorialist is advised that until near the commencement of the present century the law was that in no case of felony could the court adjourn over the night. The object of that rule was, according to Lord Chief Justice Eyre, ' that it may be quite sure that justice will be done both to the Crown and to the prisoner ; that there should be no opportunity of having intercourse with the jury ; and that there may be no improper influence upon the minds of those who are in any manner to take a part in the decision of the cause' (Colbett's ' State Trials,' vol. 25, page 130). The first case of a trial for felony in which the Court adjourned over the night was, your memorialist is advised, that of the Queen v. Hardy (24 ' State Trials,' 414), and in that case, in order to prevent any possibility of the jury communicating with the outside public, beds were supplied for them in the courthouse, and they spent the night there. The present practice of sending jurors to an inn arose, your memorialist is advised, for the first time in the case of the Qneen v. Tooke (' State Trials,' vol. 25, page 13, et seq). In that case the Lord Chief Baron Macdonald justified the departure from the ancient form in the following words :—' But if you can preserve the spirit and are forced by physical necessity to make the form bend, it does not seem to me that the sacred principle of law is materially trenched upon if the jury continue inaccessible. . . . If the rule of law cannot be preserved consistent with physical necessity, it seems to me the court is justified in deviating from the particular mode that has obtained, ' taking care that the jury do continue inaccessible.'

" 10.   The principle thus laid down by Chief Baron Macdonald has, your memorialist submits, ever since been acted upon. When cases of felony run into a second day the jury has been sent to an inn for the night; but elaborate precautions have always been taken by those sworn by the court to take charge of the jury to secure that the jury shall be as inaccessible to the general public while in the inn as when shut up in the jury box. ‘ The sacred principle of law, the inaccessibility of the jurors,' is jealously guarded by the oath administered to the bailiffs.   It is submitted that in the present case the inaccessibility of the jury was not preserved, as the jury were allowed to go whither they pleased through the hotel—as half their number spent over three hours in the public billiard-room mixing and conversing with the members of the general public who entered the room and separated from their fellows.   It is respectfully submitted to your Excellency, that in this case the confinement of the jury in the hotel was ineffectual ; that for all purposes of separation from the outside public they may as well have dispersed to their homes as remain in the hotel ; that, in short, what Chief Baron Macdonald called ‘ the sacred principle of law—the inaccessibility of the jury,' was not observed.

" 11.   Your Excellency's attention is respectfully drawn to the fact that there are many instances in which the prerogative of the Executive has been used to prevent the execution of the sentence where irregularities have been proved to have occurred in the jury-room.   Your Excellency's attention is respectfully directed to the very recent case of Gerald Mainwaring, who, at the Summer assizes of Derby in the year 1879, was found guilty of wilful murder by a jury and sentenced to death.   It afterwards transpired that six of the jury were for a verdict of man-slaughter and six for a verdict of murder, and that a casting vote of the foreman of the jury had decided the matter.   In that case, when Sir Richard Cross, the then Home Secretary, was questioned in the House of Commons as to whether, owing to the irregularities of the jury, the capital sentence would be carried out, Sir Richard Cross said, in reply, ‘ He should have thought it absolutely unnecessary to put such a question.' (Hansard, Vol, 149, page 676.)   Mainwaring's sentence was forthwith commuted.

" 12.   There have also been cases in which the judges, when they discovered that such irregularities occurred, declined to accept the verdict.   For example, a case of the Queen v. Gilligan will be found reported in the Dublin papers of the 26th July, 1867.   In that case a woman was tried for child murder at the Tullamore assizes, the presiding judge being the late Lord Chief Baron Pigot.   It was discovered during the course of the case that at luncheon time eight of the jurors had left the box, and had gone into a refreshment room which was open to the public, but which was within the precincts of the court-house. The Lord Chief Baron commented strongly upon the conduct of the jury, fined each of them and discharged them from giving a verdict. The woman was subsequently tried on a second indictment, and found guilty of concealing the birth of her child.

"18. In the case of inferior courts the Queen's Bench has not hesitated to quash verdicts when the jury was guilty of irregularities or misconduct. Your Excellency's attention is respectfully directed to the case of the Ballyragget inquest, in which judgment was given by the Court of Queen's Bench in Ireland on the 6th day of March, 1882. In that case a verdict of wilful murder was returned by a coroner's jury, sitting at Ballyragget, in the county of Kilkenny, against two sub-inspectors of police named Bouchier and O'Brien. The Attorney-General moved the Court of Queen's Bench to quash the inquisition, on the ground that ' it had not been taken and held as by law required ; that the jurors empanelled on the inquest had, during 'the proceedings, communed with persons who were not their fellow-jurors, and with whom it was not lawful for them to communicate ; that certain of the jurors absented themselves during the examination of some of the witnesses, and did not hear the said witnesses examined ; also, that after the evidence had concluded, and after the jury had been charged by the coroner, while they were deliberating on their verdict the coroner and his son—the latter not being a juror —remained shut up with the jury during their deliberation. The communications of the jury with persons not jurors was, your memorialist is advised, one of the main reasons relied on by the Crown for quashing the inquisition. After full argument the Court of Queen's Bench made an order quashing the inquisition, and the accused parties were thus freed from the verdict. A coroner's jury is in the nature of a grand jury ; it decides nothing, but merely presents a case for inquiry. If the irregularity or misconduct of a coroner's jury is a matter so serious that their verdict is quashed and the persons accused by it allowed to go free, it is humbly submitted that the case is surely far stronger in the case of the irregularity or the misconduct of a jury finally deciding on the life or death of a human being.

"Upon these grounds and for these reasons your memorialist humbly prays that the capital sentence on the said Francis Hynes should not under the circumstances aforesaid be carried into effect. And your memorialist will, as in duty bound, ever pray.

"JOHN FROST."

Dublin : Printed by W. J. ALLEY & Co., 9 Ryder's Row, Capel Street.

www.ingramcontent.com/pod-product-compliance
Lightning Source LLC
Chambersburg PA
CBHW032248080426
42735CB00008B/1045